Improve Your Vocabulary

Other Books on

WORD POWER SERIES

1. Effective English Comprehension Read Fast, Understand Better ! **(New)**
2. Latest Essays for College & Competitive Examinations **(New)**
3. Dictionary of New Words **(New)**
4. Art of English Conversation Speak English Fluently **(New)**
5. Teach Yourself English Grammar & Composition **(New)**
6. Common & Uncommon Proverbs **(New)**
7. Effective Editing Help Yourself in Becoming a Good Editor **(New)**
8. Effective English A Boon for Learners **(New)**
9. Essays for Primary Classes
10. Essays for Junior Classes
11. Essays for Senior Classes
12. Dictionary of Synonyms and Antonyms
13. Dictionary of Idioms and Phrases
14. Common Phrases
15. How to Write & Speak Correct English
16. Meaningful Quotes
17. Punctuation Book
18. Top School Essays
19. How to Write Business Letters with CD
20. Everyday Grammar
21. Everyday Conversation
22. Letters for All Occasions
23. School Essays & Letters for Juniors
24. Common Mistakes in English
25. The Power of Writing
26. Learn English in 21 Lessons
27. First English Dictionary
28. Boost Your Spelling Power
29. Self-Help to English Conversation
30. The Art of Effective Communication
31. A Book of Proverbs & Quotations
32. Word Power Made Easy
33. English Grammar Easier Way
34. General English for Competitive Examinations
35. Spoken English
36. School Essays, Letters Writing and Phrases
37. How to Write & Speak Better English
38. Quote Unquote (A Handbook of Famous Quotations)
39. Improve Your Vocabulary
40. Common Errors in English
41. The Art of Effective Letter Writing
42. Synonyms & Antonyms
43. Idioms
44. Business Letters

Improve Your Vocabulary

James Willaims

4735/22, Prakash Deep Building
Ansari Road, Darya Ganj,
New Delhi - 110002

Lotus Press : Publishers & Distributors
Unit No. 220, 2nd Floor, 4735/22, Prakash Deep Building,
Ansari Road, Darya Ganj, New Delhi- 110002
Ph.: 41325510, 98118-38000
• E-mail : lotuspress1984@gmail.com
www.lotuspress.co.in

Improve Your Vocabulary

ISBN: 81-89093-96-7

Printed & Published by : **Lotus Press Publisher & Distributors,** New Delhi-02

CONTENTS

Preface

The purpose of this book is to help you master the English language quickly, easily and thoroughly. It will help you to become a good speaker or writer if you are a poor one, or become a better one if you are a good speaker and writer.

This book teaches you thousands of words to add to your vocabulary, and gives you all the clear explanations, simple rules, and professional tips for vocabulary building.

As shown by actual tests, a person's success in any field is closely related to his or her vocabulary and language skills. Such tests show that successful executives, students, scientists, secretaries, housewives, doctors — successful people in all walks of life — all have in common a mastery of words. That is why this book can be important to you. It can teach you to use your language far more easily, correctly and effectively than you do now. It offers you the kind of self-training that can make you a confident, persuasive speaker and writer.

This book forms a complete self-teaching and review book on vocabulary building and good English. It contains step-by-step chapters that give you important vocabulary words and all the facts and easy-to-remember rules, hints and tips you need to know. Each teaches you vocabulary building and the do's and don't's of good English. Each is complete, authoritative, and full of information, word lists, and entertaining special features.

Every chapter gives you concise, easy-to-remember explanations of one basic group of vocabulary words or of one basic problem in English. Most chapters contain lists of words to add to your vocabulary.

A large, useful vocabulary is the basis of word power. It takes up three keys — roots, prefixes and suffixes — to vocabulary building by teaching you to recognise the basic building blocks of words, while at the same time teaching you thousands of words using these building blocks.

However much time you take to study, read, browse in, or refer to this book, remember one thing: you will be mastering the English language — there are not many more profitable or satisfying ways to spend your time.

1

RootS

Words evolve in curious and different ways. The quickest, most useful, and easiest way to increase your word power is to analyse and understand how words are put together. Once you learn to recognise the building blocks with which words are made, many previously unfamiliar words become meaningful and useful.

You will find that many words are actually made up of related or identical parts that you already know. For example, most people use the word *salary* and its plural form, *salaries*. They also recognise the word *salaried,* meaning 'paying a salary'— *He has a salaried job at the museum* — or 'receiving a salary' — *How many salaried salesmen does the company employ?*

The word *salary* is based on the Latin root *sal-* meaning 'salt'. Roman soldiers were given a special allowance to buy their own salt. That is why the expression 'He is not worth his salt' means 'He is not worth his pay'.

Let us go deeper into this root *sal-*. What do we put salt on? Salads. What is highly salted, spiced meat? Salami. What do chemists call water, soil or solution containing salt? *Saline.* So, if you learn one basic word or one basic root, you can instantly increase your sight vocabulary.

Many Latin and Greek words and roots have been absorbed into the English language. These roots are building blocks which are limited in number and simple in meaning. You can use them in analysing, understanding and using thousands of words almost on sight. These simple units are often not words themselves, but are combined with other elements to form words.

A root of a word never changes, even though other letters or word parts may be added to it at the beginning or the end.

Examples : revive, vital, vitamin, vital, vivid, viviparous, vivacious.

Each of these words is built on the building block of *vit-* or *viv-,* meaning 'life' or 'to live'. This part is called a root. In the above examples, the roots are used in combination with other word-building blocks such as prefixes, which come at the beginning of a word (*re-* meaning 'again' in the first word *revive*), and suffixes, which come at the end of a word. In each word the root is the foundation, the basic building block.

Once you know a root and some of the words built on it, you can keep building. Let us analyse the words from the various roots to see how they are all built up.

ROOT: AC, ACR, ACU

The Latin root *acu* or *acr* means 'sharp'. You should sharpen your vocabulary with the following core words.

acrid

This comes from *acr,* meaning 'sharp', and the Latin suffix *id* meaning 'with a particular quality'. Thus, *acrid* means 'having a sharp quality in smells and tastes; Bitter or burning to the senses'.

Example: The acrid smoke hurt our eyes.

The word *acrid* used here is an adjective, and the noun form of it is *acridity.*

Example: The acridity of the smoke made our eyes water.

acrimony

This comes from *acr* meaning 'sharp', and the Latin suffix *mony*, meaning 'quality of being'. To be more specific, *acrimony* means 'sharpness of speech or temper'.

Example: Our quarrel was full of acrimony.

The word *acrimony* is a noun, the adjective form of which is *acrimonious*, meaning 'full of bitterness; sharp; sarcastic'.

Example: Their discussion turned into an acrimonious debate.

acuity

This word is made up of *acu*, and the Latin suffix *ity* which means 'the state, condition or quality of being'. Thus *acuity* means 'sharpness of mind and quickness of understanding'.

Example: The professor has great mental acuity.

acumen

This comes directly from a Latin word meaning 'sharpness of mindness; intelligence; shrewdness'.

Example: Meera has shown great acumen in her judgment of the case.

acute

This word stems from a Latin word meaning 'sharpened' or 'coming to a sharp point'. Hence the word came to mean 'reaching a crisis; critical; keen; intense; violent' and also 'intense to a point'. The following examples will bring out clearly the various meanings.

Examples

1. An *acute* angle is an angle of less than 90 degrees.
2. He is suffering from *acute* appendicitis.
3. The food shortage in the village is becoming *acute*.

4. The boy has a quick, *acute* mind.
5. The sprain in the leg was causing *acute* pain.

The word *acute* is an adjective, and the word based on it, *acutely,* is an adverb.

Example: He was acutely conscious of their hostile looks.

acid

This is from the Latin adjective *acidus,* meaning 'sharp; sour'. It has the same root as *acer* meaning 'keen; sharp'.

Example: He used a few drops of acid to clear the stains.

Vinegar has an acid taste. From *acid* come words such as *acidify* (verb) and *acidity* (noun).

Example: Don't allow the conversation to acidify into bitterness. He is suffering from acidity of the stomach.

acerbic

This word means 'harsh and sharp'. It also means 'bitter and cutting'.

Example: Acerbic comments might be made during an acrimonious dispute.

acupuncture

This is a medical term which means a method of pricking the tissues of the human body with fine needles in order to cure a disease, to relieve pain, or as a local anaesthetic.

ROOT : AG, ACT

The Latin *ag* or *act* means 'to do; drive'. This root forms some of the most frequently used words in the English language. Some common words are *act* and *action.* The following are some more examples.

agenda

This word comes directly from a Latin word based on *ag* meaning 'to do', and means 'a list of things to be done; a list of things to be discussed or decided upon'.

Example: What is the next item on the agenda?

agent

This, derived from *ag*- meaning 'to do' plus the Latin suffix *ent,* who means 'a person who acts for other people'. This word applies to one who does a specific action or job, or who works for or represents an individual, company or government bureau.

Examples

1. He is an FBI agent.
2. Does he have a press agent?
3. Do they have a sales agent in our town?

Agency based on *agent,* means 'a company, business or place of business providing a specified service'.

Example: We have an advertising agency here.

agile

Made up of *ag* meaning 'to do' and the Latin suffix *ile* meaning 'pertaining to; like; having the character or quality of' means 'able to move quickly and easily; active; nimble'.

Example: This kid is agile as a monkey.

A word based on *agile* is *agility,* meaning 'the ability to move quickly and easily'.

Example: That fat lady has remarkable agility!

active

This comes from *act* meaning 'to do' plus the Latin suffix *ive* meaning 'inclined to; tending to; having the character quality of'. Thus, *active* means 'inclined to action; working; busy; lively'.

Example: She takes an active part in politics.

The adjective *active* become *activate* as verb and *activity* as noun. *Activity* means 'busy or energetic action', or 'being active or lively'. *Actuate* means 'to make active or make capable of action'.

Examples

1. The house has been full of activity all day.
2. Sailing is an activity I much enjoy.
3. The burglar alarm was activated by mistake.

actor

This word is formed from *act* meaning 'to do' and the Latin suffix *or* meaning 'a person who does something' or 'a person who acts'.

Example: The actor in the play is quite popular in this area.

While *actor* is masculine, its faminine form is *actress.*

actual

This comes from the Latin word *actus,* 'a doing', which is based on *act* meaning 'to do', and the Latin suffix *al* which means 'pertaining to; characterised by'. *Actual* means 'existing in fact; real'.

Example: What were his actual words?

Actually, an adverb, and *actuality,* a noun, are two words based on *actual.* While *actually* means 'really; in fact', *actuality* means 'actual existence; reality'.

Examples

1. What did he actually say?
2. Our dream of reaching the moon has become an actuality.

enact

This word is derived from the Latin prefix *en* meaning 'to make; cause to be', and the Latin root *act* means 'perform a role on, or as if on, the stage of a theatre' or 'make or pass a decree'.

Example

1. This is a one-act drama enacted by children.
2. The new bill was recently enacted by Parliament.

The noun form of the verb *enact* is *enactment,* meaning 'the passing of a law' or 'a law that has been passed'.

Example: The enactment of the new bill has drawn a lot of criticism from the public.

ROOT: AM

The Latin *am* means 'to love'. Some examples with this root are: amateur, amatory, amiable, amicable, etc.

amateur

This word comes from *am* meaning 'to love' and the French suffix *ateur* which means 'a person who'. Thus, an *amateur* is 'a person who practises sport or artistic skill without receiving money; a person who is unskilled or inexperienced in an activity'.

Examples

1. Although he is an amateur, he is a first-class player.
2. I did not employ them as they were just a bunch of amateurs.

amatory

This comes from the Latin word based on the root *am* meaning 'to love', and the Latin suffix *ory* meaning 'related to; like; resembling'. Thus, *amatory* means 'relating to or inspired by sexual love'.

Example: The library is full of amatory literature.

amiable

This stems from *am* meaning 'to love', and the Latin suffix *able* meaning 'able to; capable of; worthy of. Thus, *amiable* means showing and inspiring friendliness; pleasant and good tempered'.

Example: He is an amiable person.

The noun form of the adjective *amiable* is *amiability,* meaning 'the quality or state of being friendly; friendliness'.

Example: The amiability of their rivalry impressed us.

amicable

This comes from the Latin word as *amiable* and contains the same root and suffix, although the spelling is different. *Amicable,* though also meaning 'friendly', means 'showing friendliness; without hostility'.

Example: An amicable settlement was reached.

Amicably, an adverb, means 'in a friendly, peaceable manner' and *amicability,* a noun, means 'the quality or state of being amicable; friendliness; peaceableness'.

Examples

1. They lived together amicably for several years.
2. The amicability of their parting was remarkable.

amorous

This is a combination of *am* meaning 'to love' and the Latin suffix *ous* meaning 'full of; given to; having, or like'. *Amorous* thus means 'showing or feeling love; relating to love'.

Example: He became quite amorous at the office party.

enamoured

This stems from the Latin prefix *en* meaning 'to make; cause to be' plus the root *am* meaning 'to love' and the suffix *ed* meaning that the word is a past participle. *Enamoured* means 'fond of or delighted by something'.

Example: He was enamoured of the sound of his own voice.

ROOT : ANIM

The Latin root *anim* means 'life; mind; soul; spirit'. This root appears in several important words like animal, animosity, unanimous, equanimity, etc.

animal

It comes from *anim* meaning 'life' plus the Latin suffix *al* meaning 'pertaining to, characterised by.' Thus, *animal* means that which is characterised by life, a living being'. It also means 'any creature other than man' or 'any creature other than a man, bird, fish or insect'.

Example: A dog is a faithful animal.

Two words based on animal are *animality*, a noun, and *animalistic*, an adjective. *Animality* means 'animal nature; the nature and qualities of an animal', and *animalistic* means 'resembling an animal; like an animal'.

Examples

1. Some men should subdue the animality in their natures.
2. His rude behaviour was more animalistic than human.

animate

This comes from *anim* meaning 'life' the Latin suffix *ate* which means 'having; being'. *Animate* means 'to give life to; make lively'.

Example: A smile animated her face.

Three words based on *animate* are *animated* (adjective), *animation* (noun) and *inanimate* (adjective). *Animated* means 'lively', *animation* means 'liveliness; vivacity', and *inanimate* means 'lifeless'.

Examples

1. I had rarely seen him so animated.
2. We could see how excited he was, by the animation in his face.
3. A stone is an inanimate object.

equanimity

This is derived from the Latin root *equ* meaning 'equal; even; and the root *anim* meaning 'mind' plus the Latin suffix *ity* meaning 'the state, condition or quality of'. Thus, *equanimity* means 'calmness of mind or temper'.

Example: Nothing disturbs his equanimity.

A word based on *equanimity,* a noun, is *equanimous,* an adjective, meaning 'even tempered'.

Example: The judge was a good-natured, equanimous man.

magnanimity

This word is made up of the Latin root *magn* meaning 'great' and the root *anim* meaning 'mind; spirit' plus *ity* meaning the state, condition or quality of'. Thus, *magnanimity* means 'greatness of mind or spirit; the quality of being high-minded'.

Example: He showed great magnanimity towards his opponent.

A word based on the noun *magnanimity* is the adjective *magnanimous* meaning 'having or showing great generosity'.

Example: He was a leader who was magnanimous in victory.

unanimous

This comes from the Latin root *un* meaning 'one' and the root *anim* meaning 'mind' plus the Latin suffix *ous* which means 'having; being'. Thus, *unimous* means 'all agreeing on a decision or an opinion' or 'of a decision given or held by everybody'.

Examples

1. The villagers are unanimous in their opposition to the building of a dam.
2. He was elected by a unanimous vote.

A word based on the adjective *unanimous* is the noun *unanimity* meaning 'complete agreement or unity'.

Example: The jury reached unanimity on the question of his guilt.

ROOT : ANNU, ENNI

The Latin root *annu* or *enni* means 'year'. Some examples are annual, perennial, centennial, annuity, etc.

annals

It comes from the root *annu-* meaning 'year' and the Latin suffix *al* meaning 'of; pertaining to'. Basically *annals* means 'yearly records', but its use has been expanded to mean 'records in general' and especially 'historical record'.

Example: His is a name that will go down in the annals.

annual

This comes from *annu* meaning 'year' and the Latin suffix *al* meaning 'of; pertaining to'. *Annual* means 'happening every year' or 'calculated for the year'.

Examples

1. The circus here is an annual event.
2. Let us check your annual income.

perennial

This comes from the Latin prefix *pre* meaning 'through' plus *enni* meaning 'year'. Hence, perennial means 'lasting for a long time' or 'constantly recurring'.

Examples

1. Romance is a perennial subject of interest.
2. Leakage in the bathroom is a perennial problem.

centennial

This is formed from the Latin root *cent* meaning 'one hundred' and *enni* meaning 'year'. Thus, *centennial* means 'occurring every 100 years'.

Example: The company recently celebrated its centennial anniversary.

annuity

This is formed from *annu* meaning 'year' and the Latin suffix *ity* meaning 'the state, condition or quality of being'. Hence, *annuity* means 'a fixed sum of money paid to one yearly'.

Example: So far she has been receiving a modest annuity.

ROOT : ANTHROP, ANTHROPO

The Greek word *anthrop-* or *anthropo-* means 'man; human'.

anthropology

This comes from *anthropo* meaning 'man; human' plus the greek root *ology* meaning 'the science or study of'. Thus, *anthropology* means the study of mankind, especially of its origins, development, customs and beliefs.

Examples: Anthropology is a subject that is more interesting than sociology.

A word based on *anthropology* is *anthiopologist* meaning 'a person who is an expert in anthropology'.

philanthropist

This comes from the Greek root *phil* meaning 'love' and *anthrop* meaning 'man; human' plus the Greek suffix *ist* meaning 'a person who believes in; a person engaged in'. Thus, a *philanthropist* is 'a person who helps others, especially through charitable work or donations of money'.

Example: The university was founded by a millionaire philanthropist.

Philanthropy means 'concern for the welfare of mankind; benevolence', while *philanthropic* means 'of or inspired by philanthropy'.

Examples

1. He is a man known for his philanthropy.
2. He was guided in his actions b) philanthropic motives.

misanthrope

This is made up of the Greek root *mis* meaning 'hate, hatred' and *anthrop* meaning 'man; humans'. Thus, a *misanthrope* is 'a person who hates mankind and avoids human society.'

Example: It is impossible for a misanthrope to be a philanthropist.

Misanthropist means exactly the same thing (a person who hates his fellowmen); *misanthiopic,* means 'feeling or showing hatred for one's fellowmen'; and *misanthropy,* means 'hatred of mindkind'.

ROOT : CAD, CAS, CID

The Latin root *cad, cid* or *cas* means 'to fall; befall; happen by chance'. Even though it has three spellings, this is one root. This root is used to form several basic works in English.

accident

It comes from the Latin prefix *ad* or *ac* meaning 'to; upon' and the root *cid* meaning 'to fall; befall; happens, by chance' plus the Latin suffix *ent*, which is the same as the English suffix *ing*. Thus, *accident* means 'something that happens to someone by chance, an unexpected happening without a cause or plan; a chance; a mishap'.

Examples

1. He was killed in a road accident.
2. By accident of birth he is entitled to Australian citizenship.
3. I only found it by accident.

casual

This comes from *cas* meaning 'to fall; befall, happen by chance' and the suffix *al* meaning 'of; like; pertaining to.' Thus *casual* means 'like that which happens by chance; offhand; informal; not planned or serious'.

Examples

1. This is just a casual encounter.
2. His attitude to his job is rather casual.
3. He had a casual glance at the book.

A word based on *casual* is *casualty,* meaning 'a person or thing that is hurt or destroyed by chance, as in an accident' or 'an accident'.

Examples

1. The cottage was a casualty of the forest fire.
2. Heavy casualties were reported in the war.

A *casual* meeting happens by chance. *Casual* work is work that you happen just to 'fall into'. A *casualty* is someone who 'falls' in a battle or accident.

decadent

This derives from the Latin prefix *de* meaning 'down' and the root *cad* meaning 'to fall' plus the suffix *ent,* which is the same as the English suffix *ing*. Thus, *decadent* means 'falling into ruin; falling down morally; declining; decaying'.

Example: Roman society became decadent before the fall of the Empire.

Decadent means literally 'falling down', but in a moral or cultural sense.

A word related to *decadent* is *decay* meaning 'falling into ruin' or 'to decline, rot or decompose'.

Examples

1. Sugar decays your teeth.
2. Our powers decay in old age.

incident

This comes from the Latin prefix *in* meaning 'on; upon' and *cid*meaning 'to fall; happen by chance' plus the suffix *ent,* which is the same as the English suffix *ing*. Thus, *incident* means 'an event or occurrence' or 'something that happened'.

Examples

1. The old man told about an interesting incident in his past.
2. An incident at the border of the two countries led to war.

Three words based on *incident* are *incidence, incidental,* and *incidentally. Incidence* means 'the degree of occurrence; the frequency with which something happens' *incidental* means 'occurring in the course of something else; secondary; casual'. *incidentally* means 'by the way'.

Examples

1. This area has a high incidence of crime.
2. He has additional responsibilities that are incidental to the job.
3. Some people, and incidentally that includes Sonia, just look after themselves properly.

occident

This comes from the Latin prefix *oc* meaning 'toward' and the root *cid* meaning 'to fall' plus the suffix *ent,* which is the same as the English *ing.* Thus, *occident* means 'that which is toward the falling (or setting) sun'; hence, 'the West; the Western Hemisphere'.

Example: The Occident is the opposite of the Orient.

A word base on *occident* is *occidental,* which means 'of or belonging to the West; belonging to the countries in the western hemisphere'.

It may also mean 'a person born or living in a western country'.

Example: Marco Polo was an Occidental who visited the Orient.

occasion

This is made up of the Latin prefix *oc* meaning 'toward' and *cas* meaning 'to fall'. *Occasion* originally meant 'a falling toward, as an opportunity'; it now means 'a favourable time, the time of an event, the event itself or the reason for it'.

Example: The wedding was quite an occasion.

A word based on *occasion* is *occasional,* which means 'happening irregularly or now and then'; or 'suiting a particular occasion'; or 'small and not part of a set'.

Examples

1. He pays me occasional visits.
2. This is an occasional music for a royal wedding.
3. This is my favourite occasional chain.

ROOT : CED, CEDE, CEED, CESS

The Latin root *ced, cede, ceed* or *cess* means 'to go; yield'. This root is used in many common and important English words. When you learn that words having *ced, cede, ceed* or *cess* in them are quickly related in meaning, you will be able to expand your vocabulary quickly.

antecedent

It comes from the Latin prefix *ante* meaning 'before' and *ced* meaning 'to go' plus the Latin suffix *ent,* which is the same as the English suffix *ing.* Thus, *antecedent* means 'going before' or 'someone or something that goes before or precedes'.

Examples: Henry IV was antecedent to Henry V.

concede

It is formed from the Latin prefix *con* meaning 'thoroughly; utterly', and *cede* meaning 'to go; yield'. Thus, *concede* means 'yielding or giving up completely', or 'admit that something is true'.

Examples

1. England conceded a goal in the first minute.
2. I was forced to concede that she might be right.

A word based on *concede* is *concession,* meaning 'thing granted or yielded after discussion'; or 'price reduction for certain categories of people'.

Examples

1. Employers made concessions to the workers in negotiations.
2. He has special concessions on all fares for old people.

exceed

This comes from the Latin prefix *ex* meaning 'beyond' and *ceed* meaning 'to go', Thus, *exceed* means 'to go beyond; surpass'.

Example: Their success exceeded all expectations.

A word based on *exceed* is *exceedingly,* meaning 'extremely'.

Example: This is an exceedingly difficult problem.

excess

This is made up of *ex* meaning 'beyond' and *cess* meaning 'to go'. Thus, *excess* means 'a going beyond what is necessary or proper, or 'an immoderate amount'; 'a surplus'. It also means 'surplus; extra; excessive'.

Examples

1. An excess of fat in one's diet can lead to heart disease.
2. She was charged an excess of Rs 200 over the amount stated on the bill.
3. Avoid excess in all things.

A word based on *excess* is *excessive,* meaning 'too much or too great; extreme; inordinate'.

Example: She has an excessive enthusiasm for music.

precede

It comes from the Latin prefix *pre* meaning 'before' and *cede* meaning 'to go'. Thus, *precede* means 'to go before or in front of'.

Example: The mayor entered, preceded by members of the council.

Two words based on *precede* are *precedence* which means 'the act or right of going before; priority'; and *precedent,* meaning 'a past act or instance that can be used as a guide for future actions'.

Examples

1. The longest-serving officer always takes precedence.
2. There is no precedent for such an action.

proceed

This comes from the Latin prefix *pro* meaning 'forward' and *ceed* meaning 'to go'. Thus *proceed* means 'go to further or the next stage; go on' or 'make one's way; go'.

Examples

1. Let us proceed to the next item on the agend.
2. I shall proceed now in a northerly direction.

Five words based on *proceed* are *proceeding, proceedings, proceeds, procedure* and *procedural. Proceeding* means 'a course of continuing action'.

Example: There was a strange proceeding on his part.

Proceedings are 'what takes place at a meeting, ceremony, etc'.

Example: The proceedings were interrupted by the fire alarm.

Proceeds are the 'useful or material results of an action or course; the return or yield'.

Example: They gave a concert and donated the proceeds to charity.

Procedure means 'manner of proceeding or going forward'; or 'a course of action'.

Example: What is the procedure for opening a bank account?

Procedural means 'of or pertaining to procedure'. The business of the committee was delayed by procedural difficulties.

Do not confuse *precede* and *proceed. Precede* contains *pre* meaning 'before' and means 'to go before or in front of'. *Proceed* contains *pro* meaning 'forward' and means 'to go forward; continue or begin'.

process

This is formed from the Latin prefix *pro* meaning 'forward' and *cess* meaning 'to go'. Thus, *process* means 'a forward movement or ongoing operation' or 'a method of producing something' or 'a series of actions that bring about a result'.

Examples

1. Teaching him Greek was a painful process.
2. They have developed a new process of making cheese.
3. Her digestive processes are very poor.

Two words based on *process* are *procession,* meaning 'a parade or continued forward movement of people, vehicles or events'; and *processional,* which means 'of or pertaining to a procession' or 'the music played or sung during a procession'.

Examples

1. A procession of visitor came to the house.
2. What is the name of the processional hymn?

recede

This comes from the Latin prefix *re* meaning 'back' and *cede* meaning 'to go'. Thus, *recede* means 'to move back from a previous position or away from an observer'.

Example: As the tide receded we were able to look for shells.

A word based on *recede* is *receding,* which means 'going or sloping back'.

Example: Tom has a receding hairline.

recess

This is made up of the Latin prefix *re* meaning 'back' and *cess* meaning 'to go'. Recess means 'an indentation or cavity' or 'a time of withdrawal'.

Examples

1. She put her umbrella in a recess near the door.
2. The court recess lasted for two hours.
3. The court recessed for two hours.

Two words based on *recess* are *recession* and *recessional. Recession* means 'movement back from a previous position; withdrawal' or 'temporary decline in economic activity or prosperity'.

Examples

1. Recently China witnessed a true recession.
2. There was gradual recession of flood waters.

Recessional means 'hymn sung as the clergy and choir withdraw after a church service' or 'pertaining to a procession'.

Example: Keeping's 'Recessional' is a splendid hymn.

ROOT : FAC, FIC, FACT, FECT

The Latin root *fac, fic, fact or fect* means 'to do; make.' It is one of the most frequently used roots in English, probably because the ideas of doing and making are so important to us.

facile

This comes from *fac* meaning 'to do; make' and the Latin suffix *ile* meaning 'able to be'. Thus, *facile* means, literally, 'able to be done'. It has come to mean 'easy to do; requiring little thought or skill'.

Note that *facile* can also mean 'too smooth and superficial to be serious'.

Examples

1. His writing is merely facile; it lacks depth.
2. Being a facile speaker, she is an effective politician.

A word based on *facile* is *facility,* which means 'ready skill or ability' or 'a building room, piece of equipment, etc., that is provided to make some action or operation easier'.

Examples

1. She has a great facility for languages.
2. The colony has facilities for sports also.

fiction

This comes from *fic* meaning 'to make' and the Latin suffix *tion* which is used to form nouns. Thus, *fiction* is literally 'a making' or 'a made-up piece of writing'. Hence, 'prose writing about imaginary characters and events'.

Example: Truth is often stranger than fiction.

Two words based on *fiction* are *fictional* which means 'pertaining or belonging to fiction; imaginary,' and *fictitious* meaning 'imaginary; not real; false'.

Examples

1. This is a fictional account of life on a farm.
2. The account of his childhood is quite fictitious.

efficient

This comes from the Latin prefix *ef* meaning 'out' and *fic* meaning 'to do; make' plus the Latin suffix *ent* which is the same as the English *ing*. Thus, efficient means 'producing a satisfactory result without wasting time or energy'.

Example: He is efficient at his job.

A word based on *efficient* is *efficiency,* meaning 'the quality of being efficient or of producing results; effectiveness'.

Example: Efficiency is the hallmark of a good secretary.

infect

It comes from the Latin prefix *in* meaning 'in' and *fect* meaning 'to do; make'. Thus, *infect* literally means 'to do into or inside of'; hence, 'to affect with a disease, contaminate'.

Example: Clean the infected area with a disinfectant.

Two words based on *infect* are *infection* and *infectious.*

Infection means 'becoming ill through contact with bacteria, etc'.

Example: The infection was checked by penicillin.

Infectious means 'caused by bacteria, etc. that are passed on from one person to another'.

Example: He is highly infectious.

manufacture

It comes from the Latin root *manu* meaning 'hand' and *fact* meaning 'to do; make' plus the Latin suffix *use* meaning 'the act of'. Thus, *manufacture* means ' make goods on a large scale using machinery' or 'invent an excuse, evidence, etc'.

Examples

1. This industry manufactures only leather goods.
2. She manufactured a false story to hide the facts.

ROOT : GEN, GENIT

The Greek and Latin root *gen* or *genit* means 'to produce; give birth to, beget'.

genesis

It comes directly from a Greek word which is based on the root *gen* meaning 'to produce; give birth to'. Hence *genesis* means 'beginning; starting point; origin'.

Example: The genesis of the universe may have been a big explosion.

genial

It comes from the Latin word as *genius* and literally means 'of one's guardian spirit'. Hence, *genial* means 'showing inborn or natural kindness or pleasantness, giving comfort, warmth or life'.

Example: She has a genial, friendly smile.

A word based on *genial* is *congenial* meaning 'sympathetic or agreeable' and used to describe people or situations that one is naturally happy with or suited to.

Example: She finds her job very congenial.

genius

This comes directly from a Latin word based on *gen* meaning 'the inborr or guardian spirit of a person or place'. Hence, *genius* came to mean 'exceptionally great mental or creative ability' or 'exceptional natural ability for something'. It also means 'a person who has a brilliant mind, especially one of great intellectual achievements'.

Examples

1. It is rare to find such genius nowadays.

2. She has a genius for languages.
3. Einstein was a mathematical genius.

genuine

This comes from a Latin word based on *gen* meaning, 'natural, inborn, innate'. Hence genuine means 'real; truly what it is said to be; not fake or artificial' or 'sincere, honest'.

Examples

1. There is no doubt that this is a genuine Rubens.
2. She seems genuine but can I trust her?

genital

This comes from *genit* meaning 'to give birth; to beget' and the Latin suffix *al* meaning 'pertaining to'. Thus, *genital* means 'of animal reproduction or reproductive organs'. The *genitals* are 'the external sexual organs'.

A word based on *genital* is *congenital,* meaning 'existing at or before birth, but not inherited' or 'by nature; natural; born'.

Examples

1. The child was born with congenital defects.
2. There is no doubt that he is a congenital idiot.

progenitor

It comes from the Latin prefix *pro* meaning 'before' and *genit* meaning 'to give birth to; beget' plus the suffix *or* meaning 'the person or thing performing the action'. Thus, *progenitor* means 'an ancestor; an originator'.

Example: Marx was the progenitor of communism.

ROOT : GRAV

The Latin root *grav* means 'heavy'. A key word to remember in learning the root *grav* is our modern adjective *grave,* meaning 'of great importance; solemn; dignified; sombre'. The word has nothing to do with the *grave* in which people are buried. That word comes from a Germanic root meaning 'to dig'. So grave means 'serious'.

Example: This is a grave economical issue.

aggravate

This comes from the Latin prefix *ag* meaning 'to' and *grav* meaning 'heavy' plus the Latin suffix *ate* which can be used to form verbs. Thus *aggravate* means 'make something worse or more serious' or 'irritate; annoy'.

Examples

1. He aggravated his condition by leaving hospital too soon.
2. He aggravates her just by looking at her.

gravity

It comes from *grave* meaning 'heavy' and the Latin suffix *ity* meaning 'the state or quality of'. Thus, *gravity* means 'force that attracts objects in space towards the centre of the planet, so that things fall to the ground when dropped' or 'importance of a worrying kind; seriousness; solemnity'.

Examples

1. Who discovered the force of gravity?
2. I don't think you realise the gravity of the situation.
3. He had a twinkle in his eye which belied the gravity of his demeanour.

Three words based on *gravity* are *gravitate, gravitation* and *gravitational.*

Gravitate means 'move towards or be attracted to somebody or something'.

Example: The conversation gravitated to cricket.

Gravitation is 'force of attraction'.

Example: The scientist was studying the effects of gravitation on bodies in space.

Gravitational means 'of or having to do with gravity or gravitation'.

Example: The earth's gravitational pull is greater than that of the moon.

ROOT : PEND, PENS

The Latin word *pend* or *pens* means 'to hang, weigh or pay'. The reason this root has three meanings is that in Roman times it referred to the weighing of gold on scales. Since weights were hung on one side of the scale and gold was weighed to determine the amount of money to pay; the root *pend* or *pens* developed all three meanings.

depend

It comes from the Latin prefix *de* meaning 'down' and *pend* meaning 'to hang'. *Depend* originally meant 'to hang down'. The modern meanings of *depend* came from the idea of something hanging down from, or being supported by, something else. Hence, *depend* means 'to rely or trust on' or 'to be determined'.

Examples

1. The children depend on their parents in many ways.
2. Whether we have the picnic or not will depend on the weather.

Three words based on *depend* are *dependable, dependence* and *dependent. Dependable* means 'that may be depended on'.

Example: I am sure you own a dependable car.

Dependence means 'trust in somebody or something; reliance on somebody or something' or 'the state of having to be supported by others' or 'the state of being affected by or needing somebody or something'.

Examples

1. I have complete dependence on her skill and experience.
2. Find a job and end your dependence on your parents.

3. The economy is based on the dependence of the crops on the weather.

Dependent means 'needing support from somebody' or 'affected or decided by something'.

Examples

1. Here is a woman with several dependent children.
2. Success is dependent on how hard you work.

dispense

This comes from the Latin prefix *dis* meaning 'away' and *pens* meaning 'to weigh'. Thus, *dispense* literally means 'to weigh and give away; hence 'to give something out; distribute' or 'prepare and give out' or 'to get along without'.

Examples

1. Every week he solemnly dispenses pocket money to each of the children.
2. The judge dispenses justice.
3. Let's dispense with these wild accusations and discuss the facts.

Three words forced on *dispense* are *dispensable, indispensable* and *dispensary.*

Dispensable means 'not necessary or essential'.

Example: A garage is useful but dispensable.

Indispensable means 'incapable of being done without; necessary; essential'.

Example: A car is indispensable to a travelling salesman.

Dispensary means 'a place where medicines or medical advice are given out'.

Example: She was a nurse at the school dispensary.

expend

This comes from the Latin prefix *ex* meaning 'out' and *pend* meaning 'to pay'. Thus, *expend* means 'to pay out; spend; use up'.

Examples

1. He is expending all his time, money and energy on this worthless project.
2. Let us not expend all our fuel now.

Five words based on *expend* are *expendable, expenditure, expense, expenses* and *expensive.*

Expendable means 'that may be consumed, destroyed, etc., to achieve a purpose'.

Example: War soldiers were considered expendable.

Expenditure means 'the action of spending' or 'amount spent'.

Examples

1. Let us review the expenditure of money on weapons.
2. Limit your expenditure to what is essential.

Expense means 'spending of money, etc; costs' .

Example: Most children in India are educated at government expense.

Expenses means 'money spent in doing a specific job, or for a specific purpose'.

Example: Who is meeting the expenses of your trip?

Expensive means 'costing a lot of money'.

Example: Houses are very expensive in this area.

suspend

This comes from the prefix *sus* meaning 'under' and *pens* meaning 'to hang'. *Suspend* literally means 'to hang something under, or from, a support above'. Hence, it means 'hang something up'; 'not allow to fall or sink in air or liquid'; 'stop temporarily'; or 'to defer action on'.

Examples

1. A lamp was suspended from the ceiling.
2. Smoke hung suspended in the still air.
3. Rail services are suspended indefinitely because of strike.
4. The judge suspended the sentence.

Three words based on *suspend* are *suspenders, suspension* and *suspense.*

Suspenders means 'suspending or being suspended', or 'system by which a vehicle is supported on its axles'.

Examples

1. The poor suspension gives a rather bumpy ride.
2. We are upset over the suspension of a pupil from school.

Suspense means 'feeling of tenseness, worry, etc., about what may happen'.

Example: Don't keep us in suspense any longer.

ROOT : SED, SID, SESS

The Latin root *sed, sid* or *sess* means 'to sit; settle'.

preside

This comes from the Latin prefix *pre* meaning 'before' and *side* meaning 'to sit'. Thus, *preside* means 'to sit before others in the place of a leader; sit in authority; act as chairman'.

Example: The major presides over the city council.

Three words based on *preside* are *president, presidency* and *presidential.*

President means 'the person chosen to preside over any organisation, group, nation, etc.; the chief executive'.

Example: The president of the committee chaired the session.

Presidency means 'office of a president'.

Example: She hopes to win the presidency.

Presidential means 'of a president or presidency'.

Example: The presidential candidate is a bachelor.

reside

This comes from the Latin prefix *re* meaning 'back' and *side* meaning 'to sit; settle'. Thus *reside* means 'to live; have one's home in a certain place' or 'to exist as a quality in something' or 'be vested in as a right'.

Examples

1. Their son resides abroad.
2. Supreme authority resides in the president.

Three words based on *reside* are *residence, resident* and *residential.*

Residence means 'a house'.

Example: Her residence is not far from her workplace.

Resident means 'a person who lives or has a home in a place, not a visitor', or 'a person in a hotel staying overnight'.

Examples

1. She is a resident of Mumbai.
2. This restaurant is open to non-residents too.

Residential means 'containing or suitable for private houses' or 'connected with or based on residence'.

Examples

1. This is a very good residential area.
2. I often go on residential summer courses.

Sediment

This comes from *sed* meaning 'to sit; settle and the Latin suffix *ment* meaning 'the act or result of'. Thus, *sediment* means 'matter that settles to the bottom of a liquid'.

Example: This wine has a gritty sediment.

session

This comes from *sess* meaning 'to sit; settle' and the Latin suffix *ment* meaning 'the act or state of'. Thus *session* means meeting or series of meetings of a parliament, lawcourt, etc., for discussing or deciding something' or 'school or university year' or 'single continuous period spent in one activity'.

Examples

1. The next session of aims negotiation will be held in Nepal.
2. The school session starts this week.
3. After several sessions at the gym, I feel a lot fitter.

ROOT : TEN, TIN, TENT, TAIN

The Latin root *ten, tin, tent* or *tain* means 'to hold'.

contain

This comes from the Latin prefix *con* meaning 'together' and *tain* meaning 'to hold'. *Contain* literally means 'to hold something together in a holder'; hence, 'to hold or have something within itself' or 'be capable of holding something' or 'keep oneself under control; keep within limits; hold back' or 'prevent something from spreading harmfully or becoming more serious' or 'subject matter'.

Examples

1. The atlas contains forty maps.
2. This barrel contains 50 litres.
3. I was so furious I couldn't contain myself.
4. Has the revolt been contained?
5. They studied the style ar d content of Shakespeare's plays.

continent

This comes from the Latin prefix *con* meaning 'together' and *tin* meaning 'to hold together, plus the Latin suffix *ent,* which is the same as our English ending *ing.* Thus, a *continent* is 'a mass of land that is holding together; one of the large land masses of the earth'.

Example: Africa is known as the dark continent.

A word based on *continent* is *continental,* meaning 'of, on, or resembling a continent' or 'pertaining to Europe or Europeans'.

Examples

1. Europe has a typical continental climate.
2. This year we are planning on a continental holiday.

detain

This comes from the Latin predix *de* meaning 'away' and *tain* meaning 'to hold'. *Detain* originally meant 'to hold away from someone that which belonged to him; to withhold freedom from someone'. Hence, *detain* means 'prevent from learning or doing something; delay' or 'keep in custody; look up'.

Examples

1. This question need not detain us long.
2. The police detained him for questioning.

A word based on *detain* is *detention,* meaning 'detaining or being detained, especially in prison' or 'punishment of being kept at school after it has closed'.

Examples

1. He was held in detention by the police.
2. The child was given two hours' detention.

lieutenant

This comes from the French word *lieu* meaning 'place' and the Latin root *ten* meaning 'to hold' plus the Latin suffix *ant* which is the same as our English ending *ing.*·*Lieutenant* literally means 'holding the place of another or acting in lieu of another'. Hence, a *lieutenant* is 'an army officer next below a captain' or 'navy officer next below a lieutenant commander' or 'officer ranking next below the one specified' or 'deputy; chief assistant'.

Examples

1. In the army, a second lieutenant ranks below a first lieutenant.
2. The lieutenant-governor inspected the scene of devastation made by tsunami.
3. His most reliable lieutenant managed the business in his absence.

pertain

This comes from the Latin prefix *per* meaning 'through; throughout' and *tain* meaning 'to hold'. *Pertain* literally means 'to have a hold throughout something'; hence, 'to have to do with or have reference to something'.

Example: This question pertains to life in seas.

Two words based on *pertain* are *pertinent* and *impertinent.*

Pertinent means 'relevant to the point'.

Example: The remarks are not pertinent to the matter we are discussing.

Impertinent means 'not respectful; rude'.

Example: It would be impertinent to suggest that he was always wrong.

pertinacious

This comes from the Latin prefix *per* meaning 'thoroughly; completely' plus the word *tenacious. Pertinacious* means 'holding firmly to an opinion or a course of action; determined'.

Example: His style of argument in meetings is not so much aggressive as pertinacious.

retain

It comes from the Latin prefix *re* meaning 'back' and *tain* meaning 'to hold'. Retain literally means 'to hold back something for oneself'; hence it means 'keep in one's possession or use' or 'continue to have; not lose' or 'keep in one's memory' or 'keep in place; hold or contain'.

Examples

1. We retained the original fireplace when we decorated the room.
2. Despite losing his job he retains his pension.
3. She retains a clear memory of the incident.
4. A dyke was built to retain the floods.

Three words based on *retain* are *retainer, retention* and *retentive.*

Retainer *means* 'fee paid to one in advance for services as and when one may need them' or 'a servant'.

Examples

1. The lawyer collected his yearly retainer from the firm.
2. The maid was an old family retainer.

tenacious

This comes from *ten* meaning 'to hold' and the Latin suffix *acious* meaning 'tending to; inclined to'. Thus, *tenacious* means 'sticking or clinging firmly together or to an object' or 'keeping a firm hold on life, principles, etc'.

Examples

1. The eagle seized its prey in a tenacious grip.
2. She is tenacious in defence of her rights.

A word based on *tenacious* is *tenacity,* meaning 'the state or quality of holding firm; stubbornness; determination'.

Example: Though badly wounded he clung to life with tenacity.

ROOT : TRACT

The important Latin root *tract* means 'to drag; draw; pull'.

attract

It comes from the Latin prefix *at* meaning 'to draw; pull'. Thus, *attract* means 'to ; toward' and *tract* meaning 'to draw; pull towards itself or oneself by unseen force' or 'arouse interest or pleasure in somebody or something' or 'arouse; prompt'.

Examples

1. A magnet attracts steel.
2. The light attracted a lot of bees.
3. The new play has attracted a good deal of criticism.

Two words based on *attract* are *attraction* and *attractive.*

Attraction means 'action or power of attracting' or 'thing that attracts'.

Examples

1. She felt an immediate attraction to him.
2. City life holds few attractions for me.

Attractive means having the power to attract:

Example: Your proposal sounds very attractive.

contract

It stems from the Latin prefix *con* meaning 'together' and *tract* meaning 'to draw; pull'. Thus, *contract* means 'to draw together; to shrink or become more compact' or 'to cause something to draw together' or 'to take on or become affected with, as a debt or a disease' or 'make a legal agreement'.

Examples

1. The pupils of his eyes contracted in the bright light.
2. Cold contracts metals.
3. He contracted large debts in his business.
4. He contracted peumonia.
5. The lawyer drew up a contract for his client.

Three words based on *contract* are *contraction, contractor* and *contractual.*

Contraction means 'becoming smaller or shorter' or 'shortened form of a word'.

Examples

1. Cold causes the contraction of metals.
2. Can't is contraction of cannot.

detract

This comes from the Latin prefix *de* meaning 'away' and *tract* meaning 'to draw'. Thus, *detract* means 'to draw or take away a part of something, as part of one's good reputation; slander'.

Example: His laziness detracts from his efficiency.

The rainy weather detracted from our enjoyment of the scenery.

Two words based on *detract* are *detractor* and *detraction.*

Detractor means 'a person who defames or disparages another'.

Example: He has always been one of the mayor's greatest detractors.

Detraction means 'a talking away of something, such as someone's good reputation; slander'.

Example: He stood firm, despite the detractions of his critics.

distract

This comes from the Latin prefix *dis* meaning 'away' and *tract* meaning 'to draw'. This *distract* means 'stop somebody concentrating on something'.

Examples: The film managed to distract me from these problems for a while.

Two words based on *distract* are *distracted* and *distraction.*

Distracted means 'unable to concentrate properly, especially because of one's strong feelings'.

Example: Distracted with anxiety he paced up and down.

Distraction means 'distracting or being distracted' or 'noise, sight' etc., that distracts the attention and prevents concentration' or 'thing or event that amuses or entertains' or 'extreme mental distress'.

Examples

1. I don't like this continuous distraction.
2. He found the noise of the photographers a distraction.
3. Television can be a welcome distraction after a hard day's work.
4. All those gory stories are a real mental distraction.

Another word having almost the same meaning as *distracted* is *distraught,* though spelt differently. *Distraught* comes from the same Latin word as *distracted,* and means 'deeply agitated in mind; worried, tense and bewildered'.

Example: She was distraught until her missing child was found.

extract

It comes from the Latin prefix *ex* meaning 'out' and *tract* meaning 'to draw; pull'. Thus, it means 'to take or get something out with effort or force' or 'obtain information, money, etc., from a person unwilling to give it' or 'obtain juices, etc. by crushing, pressing etc.' or 'substance that has been removed and concentrated' or 'a passage selected from a book, film, etc'. or 'select and present passages from a book, speech, etc'.

Examples

1. With difficulty she extracted the cork from the bottle.
2. You can extract oil from sunflower seeds.
3. The yeast extract is fresh and good.
4. She read out extracts from his letter.
5. She extracted passages for the students to translate.

A word based on *extract* is *extraction,* meaning 'action of extracting' or 'descent; parentage'.

Examples

1. We watched an extraction process at a diamond mine.
2. He is an American of Hungarian extraction.

protract

This comes from the Latin prefix *pro* meaning 'forward' and *tract* meaning 'to draw'. Thus, *protract* means 'make something last a long time or longer; lengthen or prolong'.

Example: Let us not protract the debate any further.

Two words based on *protract* are *protraction* and *protractor.*

Protraction means, 'making something last longer; extending'.

Example: Further protraction of the discussion will not achieve anything.

Protractor is an instrument for measuring and drawing angles.

Example: A protractor is used in geometry.

retract

This comes from the Latin prefix *re* meaning 'back' and *tract* meaning 'to draw; pull'. Thus, it means 'withdraw a charge, statement, etc'. or 'refuse to honour or keep an agreement, etc'. or 'move or pull something back, or in'.

Examples

1. The accused refused to retract his statement.
2. Should you not retract the offer?
3. The undercarriage on high aircraft does not always retract in flight.

Two words based on *retract* are *retractable* and *retraction.*

Retractable means 'that can be drawn in'.

Example: All the aeroplanes have wheels that are retractable.

Retraction means 'a taking back of something, especially something said or written'.

Example: He published a retraction of his unsupported accusations.

subtract

This comes from the Latin prefix *sub* meaning 'beneath; away from; under' and *tract* meaning 'draw'. Thus, it means 'take away a number or quantity away from another'.

Example: He subtracted the expenses from the profits.

A word based on *subtract* is *subtraction,* meaning 'the process of subtracting'.

Example: Subtraction is easy if you are through with your mathematics.

tract

This comes directly from the root *tract* meaning 'to draw'. The word *tract* means 'a large stretch or area of land' or 'treatment involving a continuous pull on a limb, etc'. or 'a pamphlet containing a short essay, especially on a religious or political subject'.

Examples

1. We have huge tracts of forest in this state.
2. The digestive tract seems to be clogged.
3. He wrote a number of political tracts.

traction

This comes from *tract* meaning 'draw; pull' and the Latin suffix *ion* meaning 'the act or result of'. Thus *traction* means 'the act or result of a pulling force' or 'a pulling force itself' or 'the state or condition of being subject to a pulling force' or 'the ability to grip and move on a surface without shipping'.

Examples

1. The broken leg was placed in traction to keep the parts of the fractured bone in place.
2. Trains used to be powered by steam traction.
3. It is hard for tires to get traction on an icy road.

tractor

This comes from *tract* meaning 'draw; pull; drag' and the Latin suffix *or* meaning 'a little that does'. Thus, a *tractor* is 'a thing that pulls or draws something'; hence, 'a vehicle used for pulling a piece of farm equipment, a trailor, etc'.

ROOT : VERT, VERS

The Latin root *vert* or *vers* means 'to turn'.

avert

This comes from the Latin prefix *a* meaning 'away' and *vert* meaning 'to turn'. Thus, *avert* means 'turn something away' or 'prevent; avoid'.

Examples

1. He managed to avert suspicion.
2. He averted his eyes from the terrible sight.

A word based on *avert* is *aversion,* meaning extreme dislike', literally 'that which makes one turn away'.

Example: They have an aversion to loud music.

convert

This comes from the Latin prefix *con* meaning 'thoroughly; completely' and *vert* meaning 'to turn'. Thus *convert* means 'change from one form or use to another', or 'be able to be changed from one form or use to another' or 'change one's beliefs' or 'gain extra points after scoring by kicking a goal' or 'a person converted to a different belief'.

Examples

1. A ferry was converted to carry troops during the war.
2. We have a sofa that converts into a bed.
3. He has converted to Catholicism.
4. He converted the free kick into a goal.
5. Cardinal Newman was a Catholic convert.

Eight words based on *convert* are *conversant, conversation, conversational, conversationalist, converse, conversion, converter* and *convertible.*

Conversant means 'having knowledge of something; familiar with something'.

Example: We are thoroughly conversant with all the rules.

Conversation means 'informal talk'.

Example: He was deep in conversation with his accountant.

Conversational means 'of talking'.

Example: Her limited conversational powers are a setback for her career prospects.

Conversationalist means 'a talker'.

Example: He is a good and fluent conversationalist.

Converse means 'talk' or 'the opposite' or 'statement made by reversing two elements of another statement' or 'opposite to something'.

Examples

1. She sat conversing with her guide.
2. He says she is satisfied, but I believe the converse to be true.
3. 'He is happy but not rich' is the converse of 'He is rich but not happy'.
4. They hold converse opinions.

Conversion means 'converting or being converted' or 'an instance of this'.

Examples

1. Conversion to gas central heating will save you a lot of money.
2. This is a notable building firm which specialises in house conversions.

Converter means 'a person or thing that converts'.

Example: A Bessemer converter is used to turn pig iron into steel.

Convertible means 'that can be converted' or 'a convertible thing, especially an automobile with a folding top that can be lowered or raised'.

Examples

1. Cheques are convertible into cash.
2. He drives a sedan while she uses a convertible.

divert

It stems from the Latin *di* meaning 'apart; in different directions' and *vert* meaning 'to turn'. Thus, *divert* means 'turn somebody or something from one course to another' or 'entertain or amuse'.

Examples

1. The gale diverted the ship from its course for a mile.
2. Children are easily diverted.

Three words based on *divert* are *diverse, diversion* and *diversity.*

Diverse means 'of various kinds; varied'.

Example: Her interests are very diverse.

Diversion means 'action of turning something aside or changing its direction' or 'alternative route for use by traffic when the usual road is temporarily closed' or 'entertainment activity that turns the attention from work, study etc.' or 'thing designed to draw attention away from something one does not want to be noticed'.

Examples

1. There was a diversion of flights because of fog.
2. Sorry I am late—there was a diversion.
3. It is difficult to concentrate when there are so many diversions.
4. One of the gang created a diversion in the street while the others robbed the bank.

Diversity means 'state of being varied; variety'.

Example: Now we are having a wide diversity of opinions.

reverse

This comes from the Latin prefix *re* meaning 'back' and *vers* meaning 'to turn'. *Reverse* literally means 'turned backward; having an opposite direction, character, etc'. Hence, *reverse* means 'contrary or opposite to what is expected' or 'from the end towards the start; backwards' or 'thing that is the contrary or opposite to what is expected' or 'underside or back of a coin, medal, etc.' or 'defeat' or 'control used to make a vehicle travel backwards' or 'turn made while driving backwards'.

Examples

1. In hot weather, the reverse applies.
2. This coin has a crowned lion on its reverse.
3. We suffered some serious financial reverses.
4. Put the car into reverse.
5. I can't do reverses.

Four words from *reverse* are *reversal, reversible, reversion* and *revert.*

Reversal means 'making something the opposite of what it was; turning around' or 'exchanging two positions, functions, etc'.

Examples

1. This is a dramatical reversal of her earlier decision.
2. There was a reversal of roles between husband and wife yesterday.

Reversible means 'that can be reversed'.

Example: She owns a pretty reversible coat.

Reversion means 'a return to the former condition, belief, etc.'

Example: I am surprised that they have decided on reversion to old methods.

Revert means 'return to a former state or condition' or 'return to a topic in talk or thought' or 'return or pass property, rights, etc. to the original owner, the state, etc'.

Examples

1. The fields have been reverted to moorland.

2. The conversation kept reverting to the subject of money.
3. If he dies without an heir, his property reverts to the state.

subversive

This comes from the Latin prefix *sub* meaning 'from beneath; up from under' and *ver* meaning 'to turn' plus the Latin prefix *ive* meaning 'tending to'. Thus, *subversive* means 'trying or likely to weaken or destroy a political system, an accepted belief, etc'.

Example: Was her speech subversive of law and order?

Two words based on *subversive* are *subversion* and *subvert.*

Subversion means 'the act of throwing something or the state of being overthrown'.

Example: Dictationship is the subversion of the rights of the people.

Subvert means 'destroy the authority of a political system, religious faith, etc.' or 'corrupt the morals or loyalty of'.

Examples

1. These are surely writings that subvert Christianity.
2. No doubt he is a diplomat subverted by a foreign power.

ROOT : VOLV, VOLUT

The Latin root *volv* or *volut* means 'to roll'.

evolve

This comes from the Latin prefix *e* meaning 'out' and *volv* meaning 'to roll'. Thus *evolve* means 'develop naturally and gradually' or 'develop gradually from a simple form to a complex form'.

Examples

1. He has evolved a new theory after many years of research.
2. Many Victorians were shocked by the notion that man had evolved from lower forms of life.

A word based on *evolve* is *evolution,* meaning 'the process of developing from one state to another, usually gradually' or 'anything that develops by such a process'.

Examples

1. The evolution of the aeroplane is an example of technological development.
2. The evolution of living things took place over millions of years.

involve

This comes from the Latin prefix *in* meaning 'in' and *volv* meaning 'to roll'. *Involve* literally means 'to roll in or roll up'. Thus, it means 'something necessary as a condition or result; entail' or 'include or affect somebody or something in its operation' or 'cause to take part in an activity or a situation' or 'bring one into a difficult situation'.

Examples

1. This scheme involves computers.
2. The strike involved many people.
3. Don't involve me in solving your problems.
4. He was involved in a heated argument.
5. The witness's statement involves you in the robbery.

Two words based on *involve* are *involved* and *involvement*.

Involved means 'complicated in thought or form' or 'concerned with something' or 'connected with somebody'.

Examples

1. The directions he gave us were so involved that we were lost.
2. Now he has become involved in politics.
3. He sees her often but doesn't want to get too involved.

Involvement means 'an involving or being involved'.

Example: The nightclub owner's involvement with gangsters was well known.

revolve

It comes from the Latin prefix *re* meaning 'back' and *volv* meaning 'to, all'. *Revolve* literally means 'to roll back to the starting point; roll around'. Thus, *revolve* means 'move in a circular orbit' or 'rotate' or 'centre on somebody or something'.

Examples

1. The earth revolves around the sun.
2. A wheel revolves on its axis.
3. My life revolves around my family.

Three words based on *revolve* are *revolution, revolutionary* and *revolver.*

Revolution means 'overthrow of a system of government by force' or 'complete or drastic change of method, conditions etc'. or 'revolving of one planet round another' or 'a single complete movement or turn round a central point'.

Examples

1. He has lived through two revolutions.
2. Credit cards have brought about a revolution in people's spending habits.
3. The revolution of the earth on its axis round the sun takes a year.
4. This is a record designed to be played at 45 revolutions per minute.

Revolutionary means 'of political revolution' or 'involving complete or drastic change'.

Examples

1. He is heading a revolutionary party.

2. Genetic engineering will have revolutionary consequences for mankind.

Revolver means 'pistol with a revolving chamber from which bullets are fed into the breech for firing'.

Example: Was the bullet fired from a pistol or from a revolver.

revolt

It comes from the Latin prefix *re* meaning 'back' and the root *volt,* which is based on *volv* meaning 'to roll'. Revolt literally means 'to roll back on or turn against'. Thus, *revolt* as a verb means 'to rise in rebelion against the constituted authority' or 'to disgust or repel'. As a noun, *revolt* means 'an uprising; a rebelion against authority' or 'the state of a person or persons who revolt'.

Examples

1. The colonists revolted against taxation without representation.
2. She was revolted by the strong smell of garlic.
3. Troops were dispatched to put down an armed revolt.
4. The nation was in revolt.

The following table provides the root, language of origin, meaning in original language, and English examples.

Root	*Language of Origin*	*Meaning in Original Language*	*English Examples*
ac, acu, acr	Latin	keen, sharp	acrid, acrimony, acuity, acumen, acute, acerbic, acupuncture
ag, act	Latin	do, drive	agenda, agent, agile, active, actor, actual, enact, inactive, transact
am, amat	Latin	love	amateur, amatory, amiable, amicable, amorous, enamoured
anim	Latin	life, mind, soul, spirit	animal, animate, animosity, equanimity, unanimous, magnanimity
annu, enni	Latin	year	annals, annual, erennial, centennial, annuity
anthrop, anthropo	Greek	man, human	anthropology, philanthropist, misanthrope
archae archaeo	Greek	ancient	archaeology, archaeologist
arch, archi	Greek	chief, principal	archangel, archbishop, archenemy, architect
arch, archy	Greek	ruler, government	monarch, monarchy, matriarch, matriarchy, patriarchy
aud, audi, audit	Latin	hear, examine	audible, audience, audio, audition, auditor, auditorium
aut, auto	Greek	self	autocrat, autograph, automatic, automobile
bel, belli	Latin	war	belligerent, rebel
bene, benign	Latin	well, good	benefactor, benefit, benevolent, beneficial, beneficiary
bio	Greek	life	biochemistry, biography, biology
cad, cas, cid	Latin	fall, befall by chance	accident,casual, decadent, incident, occident, occasion

cap, capt ceiv	Latin	take, seize	capable, capture, deceive, cept, except, incipient, receive, concept, deceit, recipient
carn	Latin	flesh	carnal, carnival, carnage, carnation
ced, cede, ceed, cess	Latin	go, yield	antecedent, concede, exceed, excess, precede, proceed, process, recede, recess
celer	Latin	fast, rapid	celerity, accelerate
cent	Latin	one hundred	centenary, centipede, century, percent, centenarian, centurion
cern, cret	Latin	separate, distinguish	concern, discern, secret, discrete, secretarial, secretive
clam, claim	Latin	cry out, shout	declaim, exclaim, proclaim, clamour, proclamatory, reclamation
clud, clus clos	Latin	shut, close	conclude, disclose, enclose, exclude, include, preclude
cogn	Latin	know	cognisant, cognition, recognise, incognito
cord	Latin	heart	cordial, accord, record, concord, discord
corp, corpor	Latin	body, flesh	corpulent, corpuscle, incorporate, corps, corpse, corporation
cre, cret, cresc	Latin	grow	crescent, increase, concrete, decrease, accretion, crescendo, excrescence
cred	Latin	believe, trust	credit, accredit, credentials, discredit, credible, incredible, credulous
cumb, cub	Latin	lie down	cubicle, incubate, incumbent, succumb
cur, curs cours	Latin	run, go	concur, current, occur, recur, discourse, incur, recourse

de, div	Latin	a god	deify, deity, devine
derm, dermat	Greek	skin	dermatitis, epidermis, hypodermic
dict	Latin	say, speak	contradict, dictate, diction, predict, addict, dictum, edict, interdict
doc, doct	Latin	teach	docile, doctor, doctrine, document
duc, duct	Latin	lead	conduct, introduce, produce, reduce, seduce, traduce
equ	Latin	equal, even	adequate, equilibrium, equivocal, equable, equator, equipoise, inequity
fac, fic, fact, fect	Latin	do, make	facile, fiction, efficient, fact manufacture, infect, affect, perfect, unification
fer, lat late	Latin	bear, carry	confer, differ, offer, prefer, refer, suffer, transfer, collate, relate, deferential
firm	Latin	firm	affirm, confirm, infirm
flect, flex	Latin	bend	deflect, flexible, reflect, inflection, reflex
flu, flux	Latin	flow	affluent, fluency, influence, effluent, fluid, fluent, fluctuate, flux
frung, fring, fract,	Latin	break	fraction, fragile, fragment, infringe, fracture, refract, frag frangible
fus, fund found	Latin	melt, pour	confuse, foundry, fusion, refund, diffuse, profuse, suffuse, effusive
gam	Greek	marriage	bigamy, monogamy, polygamy, gamete
gen, gener gen, genit	Latin	give birth to, beget, kind, type	gene, general, genealogy, generate, generous, genesis, genial, genius, genre, genital, ingenuous, oxygen, engine

geo	Greek	earth	geography, geology, geometry, geopolitics
ger, gest	Latin	carry, carry on, produce	belligerent, digest, gestate, congest, gesticulate, ingest, gesture
grad, gress	Latin	step, go	aggression, gradual, graduate, progress, centigrade, digression, regress, transgress
grat	Latin	pleasing	congratulate, grateful, gratify, gratitude, gratuity
grav	Latin	heavy	aggravate, gravity, grave
greg	Latin	crowd, herd	gregarious, congregate, egregious, segregate
gyn	Greek	woman	gynaecology, misogynist
her, hes	Latin	to stick	adhere, cohere, inhere, incoherent
hom, homin	Latin	human	homicide, hominoid, bonhomie, homage
jac, ject	Latin	throw, lie, stick out	abject, adjacent, conjecture, eject, inject, object, project, reject
junct, join, joint	Latin	join	adjoin, conjunction, injunction, junction
leg, lig, lect	Latin	choose, read	collect, elect, eligible, lecture, legible, select, lectern, predilection
log, logi	Greek	word, reason	logical, analogy, epilogue, prologue
loqu, locut	Latin	speak	colloquial, eloquent, elocution, interlocutor, loquacious, location
man, mani manu	Latin	hand	manual, manicure, manifest, manuscript
mater, matr	Latin	mother	maternal, matrimony, matrix, matron
mit, miss	Latin	send, let go	admit, commit, dismis, emit, permit, omit, missile, transmit, mission

mon, monit	Latin	warn, advise	admonish, monument, premonition, monitor
mov, mot,	Latin	move	emotion, promote, remote, remove, mobile, move, motion, mob
nasc, nat	Latin	be born	nascent, native, prenatal
nom, nomen, nomin	Latin	name	nominate, nominal, cognomen, misnomer
nov	Latin	new	novelty, novice, renovate
pater, patr	Latin	father, own country	paternal, paternity, repatriate, patriotic
ped	Latin	foot	pedal, pedestrian
pel, pell puls	Latin	drive, push	compel, impel, repel, pulsate, expulsion, repulsive
pend, pens	Latin	hang, weigh pay	depend, dispense, expend, suspend, pendulum, compensate, pensive
pet, petil	Latin	go, seek, strive	appitite, compete, petition repetition, impetus, impetuous
phil, philo	Greek	loving	philosophy, philanthropy, francophile
ple, plet	Latin	fill	complete, deplete, implement, replete
plic, plicit, plex, ply	Latin	fold, twist, bend, tangle connect	complex, complexion complicate, explicit, implicate, implicit, imply, replica, supplication, multiply, duplicate
pon, posit pound, pose	Latin	put, place	component, compose, composite, impose, depose, deposit, dispose, expound, compound
port	Latin	carry	deport, export, import, portable, porter
put, putat	Latin	think, reckon	putative, compute, dispute, reputation
quir, quest,	Latin	seek, ask	acquire, inquire, require,

quisit			question, conquest, inquisitive, requisite
rupt	Latin	break, burst	corrupt, disrupt, erupt, interrupt, rupture
scrib, script	Latin	write	describe, inscribe, prescribe, proscribe, subscribe, transcribe, conscript
sect	Latin	cut	section, interdect, sector, vasectomy
secut, sequ	Latin	follow	sequel, consecutive, consequence, execute
sed, sid, sess	Latin	sit, settle	preside, reside, sentiment, session, sedate, sedentary, sediment, obsess
soph	Greek	wisdom	sophistry, sophisticated, philosophy
spec, spic, spect	Latin	look, look at	conspicuous, expect, inspect, respect, spectacles, spectator, auspicious, suspect
tact, tang ting	Latin	touch	contact, contingent, intact, tact, tangible, tactile
temp, tempor	Latin	time	temporary, temporise, contemporary, extempore
ten, tin tent, tain	Latin	hold	contain, continent, detain, lieutenant, pertain, pertinacious, retain, tenacious
ter, terr	Latin	land	territory, terrace, terrestrial, interred
theo	Greek	god	theology, theocracy, apotheosis, pantheon
tract	Latin	drag, pull, draw	attract, contract, detract, distract, extract, protract, retract, subtract, traction
ven, vent	Latin	come, move toward	adventure, circumvent, convene, prevent, convenient, event, invent

ver, verac	Latin	true	veracity, verily, very, aver, verdict
vers, vert	Latin	turn	avert, convert, divert, reverse, subversive
vict, vine	Latin	defeat, win	victory, convict, convince, province
vid, vis	Latin	see	evident, provide, television videa, vision
vir	Latin	man, male	virile, virago, triumvirate
vit, vav	Latin	life, live	vital, vitamin, vivid, vivacious, convivial, revive
voc, vok	Latin	voice, call	advocate, evoke, invoke, provoke, vocabulary, vocation, vocal, vociferous
volv, volt volut	Latin	roll, turn	involve, evolve, revolve, revolt, convolvuless

2

PREFIXES

A prefix consists of a letter or group of letters placed before a root or word to alter its meaning. The word *prefix* is derived from two Latin words meaning 'to place or attach before'. Prefixes rank next in importance to roots as building blocks for a greater vocabulary.

Sometimes the same building block may seem to fit two different categories. For example, the Latin *bene* meaning 'good' is typically a prefix in position, being attached to the beginning of a word, as in *benefactor.* But *bene* actually is, and functions as, a root, since it finishes half the basic meaning of any word it forms. A *benefactor* is not simply 'one who does something' but 'one who does good'. The same thing occurs in the related word *benefit, benediction* and *benefice.* Hence, the fact that *bene* books like a prefix does not mean that we may not refer to it as a root.

The prefixes discussed in the following pages generally fall into one of four groups. The first is made up of mostly Latin and Greak words that have the meaning of English prepositions. The following are a few of them.

Ante (before), as in*antechamber,* means 'a room'. *Circum* (around), as in *circumvent,* means 'to go around or to avoid'.

Com (with, together), as in *combine,* means 'to bring together in close union; blend; merge-unite'

Intra (within, inside of), as in *intramural,* meaning 'situated or occurring within the limits of a city, building, organisation, etc'.

Sub (under), as in *substandard,* means 'below the standard; lower than the established rate or requirement'.

Super (above in position; over), as in *superstructure,* means 'the part of the ships structure above the main deck'.

Ultra (on the other side of, beyond), as in *ultramodern,* means 'extremely modern'.

The second group of prefixes servs to give a negative meaning to a word or to reverse and undo an action : *dis* (as in *disease,* literally 'a state of being not at ease; illness'); *in* (as in *incapable,* meaning 'not capable, not able to'); *mal* (as in *malfunction,* meaning 'a failure to function properly'); *mis* (as in *misinform,* which means to 'inform incorrectly; to give wrong information to'); *non* (as in *non-inflammable,* meaning 'not inflammable; not apt to catch on fire easily'); *un* (as in *unbend,* which means to 'become straight again or to relax').

The third group of prefixes have to do with amount, number or degree : *ambi* (as in *ambidextrous,* which means 'able to use both hands equally well'); *bi* (as in *bicuspid,* which means 'having two points or cusps'); *hypo* (as in *hypothyroidism,* meaning 'a condition in which the thyroid gland is underactive'); *hyper* (as in *hypercritical,* meaning 'overly critical; excessively fault-finding').

The last group consists of common English words such as *extra* (as in *extraordinary*), *out* (as in *outspoken*); *over* (as in *overweight*), and *under* (as in *underprivileged*). Since such prefixes are perfectly familiar, you will have no difficulty in working out their meanings.

A number of prefixes have 'disguises', that is, their spelling changes before roots or words beginning with certain letters.

This occurs in order to make pronunciation easier and more musical. For example, *sub* meaning 'under' becomes *sug* in *suggest; com* meaning 'with' becomes *col* in *collect.*

Given below are a few prefixes which change the meaning of words or roots.

antisocial

This is made up of the prefix *anti* meaning 'against' plus the word *social* meaning 'disposed to having friendly relations with persons living in a society' or 'having to do with society and the general good'. Therefore, *antisocial* means 'not friendly or outgoing; unserviable' or 'disruptive of society and the general good'.

Examples

1. Hermits are generally considered antisocial.
2. Robbery and assault are antisocial acts.

refund

This comes from the Latin prefix *re* meaning 'again or back', plus the Latin root *fund* meaning 'to pour'. Thus *refund* means 'to pay back money'. It also means 'the money to be paid back'.

Example: We received a refund for our unused theatre tickets.

submerge

This comes from the Latin prefix *sub* meaning 'under' and the Latin root *merge* one of whose meaning is 'to plunge'. Thus, *submerge* means 'to plunder or dive under the surface of water'.

Examples

1. The flood submerged all of the farmland in the area.
2. With a flick of his tail, the porpoise submerged.

unsound

This comes from the prefix *un* meaning 'not; opposed to' and the word *sound,* which means 'healthy or strong'. Therefore, *unsound* means 'not strong, healthy, or solid; weak'.

Examples

1. The platform was rickety and unsound.
2. He was adjudged unsound of mind.

Generally, it is easy to identify prefixes. But their final consonant often adjusts itself to be more like the sound that comes after it. Prefixes ending in *d* and *n* are the most susceptible to variations. Given below are a few detailed case studies of prefixes and the words that use them.

PREFIX : AD

The Latin prefix *ad* means 'to; toward; near; at'.

adapt

This comes from *ad* meaning 'to' and the Latin root *apt* meaning 'to fit'; thus, *adapt* means 'to fit for a new use; adjust'.

Example

1. The author adapted his novel for the stage.
2. He adapted himself easily to his new job.

Be careful not to confuse the words *adapt* and *adopt. Adopt* comes from *ad* meaning 'to' and the Latin root *opt* meaning 'to choose'. Thus, *adopt* means 'to choose or take a new relationship or a new course of action'; or 'to take up from someone else and use as one's own, as an idea' or 'to vote to accept, as a motion or committee report'.

Examples

1. The Wilsons adopted two baby boys.
2. I have decided to adopt my wife's political views.
3. We willingly adopted the chairman's recommendations.

adjacent

This derives from *ad* meaning 'at' and the Latin root *jac* meaning 'to be' plus the Latin suffix *ent,* which is the same as the English ending *ing*. Thus, *adjacent* means 'lying or located near or next to something'.

Example: Alaska is adjacent to Canada.

admire

This is formed from *ad* meaning 'at'and the Latin root *mir* meaning 'to wonder'. Thus, *admire* means 'to have esteem for'.

Example: We admired the bravery of the little boys.

The following six words also use the prefix *ad*. See how the prefix enters into the meaning of the word.

addict

A person who is enslaved by some habit, especially the use of narcotic drugs.

Example: Drug addicts can be cured.

adhere

To stick; or, follow closely.

Examples

1. The tape will not adhere to this slick surface.
2. We try to adhere to the principles of democracy.

address

To speak to; or to direct. As a noun, it means a speech or a place of residence.

Examples

1. The chairman addressed the gathering.
2. She addressed the letter carefully.
3. The president was preparing his inaugural address.
4. What is your address?

administer

To manage; or to apply or supply.

Examples

1. The prime minister administers the government.
2. The doctor administered the medicine to his patient.

adore

Literally to pray or worship. Hence it means to honour as divine; or, to love or honour with great devotion.

Examples

1. Gandhi's followers adored him.
2. George adores his wife.

advice

A view or opinion on what should be done.

Example: You should follow your doctor's advice.

PREFIX : COM

The prefix *com* means 'with; together; thoroughly'. Like the prefix *ad, com* sometimes changes its spelling depending on the letters that follow it. Thus, *com* may appear as *co, col, con* or *cor;* of these different spellings, *co* is the most frequent and important.

Three typical words using *com* or a variant of it are *combat, compatriot* and *concede.*

combat

This is derived from *com* meaning 'with' and the Latin *bat* meaning 'to fight'. Thus, to *combat* means 'to fight with; fight against; oppose in battle; resist' or 'a battle or fight'.

Examples

1. We must combat disease with better health programmes.
2. Did you see much combat during the war?

compatriot

This is formed from *com* meaning 'together' and the Latin word *patriot* meaning 'countryman'. Thus, *compatriot* means 'a fellow countryman'.

Example: I saw many of my compatriots in Europe last summer.

concede

This comes from *con* meaning 'thoroughly' and the Latin root *ced* meaning 'to yield; withdraw'. Thus, *concede* means 'to yield thoroughly on some point; to give up or grant as a right or privilege'.

Examples

1. After a long argument, Bob conceded that Jim was right.
2. Even before the votes were counted, the senator conceded the election to his opponent.

The following words use the prefix *com* or one of its variants with various roots to form different words with different meanings.

coequal

An equal of another person or thing; or, equal with one another; of the same value, size, rank, etc.

Examples

1. All the lawyers were coequals in the firm.
2. In the United States Senate, Rhode Island and Texas are coequal.

coerce

To force by means of threats, intimidation, authority, etc.

Example: The racketeer coerced the businessman into paying a bribe.

coeval

Belonging to the same age, time, or era.

Example: The Aztec empire was coeval with the reign of Henry VIII.

coexist

To exist together at the same place or time.

Example: Can democracy and communism coexist?

cohere

To stick or hold firmly together, or, be consistent.

Example: This pie crust keeps crumbling; it does not cohere.

cohort

A companion or follower.

Example: He and his cohorts started the brawl.

collaborate

To work with another person or group of persons.

Examples

1. The musician and the lyricist collaborate on writing songs.
2. Quisling was accused of collaborating with the enemy.

colleague

A fellow member of a profession, organisation, etc.

Example: He and his colleagues worked hard during the disaster.

collide

To come together with violent impact.

Example: The two buses collided at the corner.

combine

To bring or come together into a close union; blend; unite.

Example: Let us combine our efforts and get the work done.

commerce

The exchange of materials, products, etc., especially on a large scale; trade.

Example: Is there much commerce between Japan and Italy?

commit

To do; or, to place someone or something in the trust of another; or, to devote oneself to something.

Examples

1. The gangster committed many crimes.
2. The murderer was committed to a hospital for the mentally ill.
3. I was committed to my ideals.

community

A group of people living together in one location, subject to the same laws, having similar interests, etc.; or, any group united by a common characteristic or common interests.

Examples

1. Our small town is a pleasant community.
2. The business community favours the law.

compact

Pressed together; firmly united; made small or packed into a small space; or, an agreement or contract.

Examples

1. A snowball must be compact if it is to be any good.
2. Japan and Taiwan have a commercial compact.

compassion

Pity for the suffering of another; fellow feeling.

Example: She feels genuine compassion for the old and infirm.

compatible

Capable of existing together, able to get along peacefully.

Example: Your ideas are not compatible with mine.

compel

To force or urge irresistibly; or, to obtain by force.

Examples

1. The general was compelled to surrender.
2. They compelled a confession at gunpoint.

compete

To take part in a contest.

Example: He will compete in the races and hurdles.

complete

Having all needed parts; lacking nothing; or, to add a needed part or parts to; to finish.

Examples

1. I am going to order the complete dinner.
2. He completed the painting job that she had started.

complex

Having many related parts; complicated or intricate. As a noun, it means an intricate whole made up of many different but related parts.

Examples

1. Computers are complex machines.
2. The manufacturing complex covered fifty acres.

composition

A putting together of different parts, ingredients, etc., to form a whole; or a whole formed in this way; or, a written theme, essay, or piece of music.

Examples

1. This flooring is a composition of tiles and cement.
2. The student's composition was neatly written.

compress

To condense; or, to press together or into a smaller space. As a noun, it means a cloth used to apply cold, heat or pressure to a part of the body.

Examples

1. Compress this report into two pages.
2. The machine compresses cotton into bales.
3. She placed a compress on the cut.

concave

Hollow and curving inward. Its opposite is convex.

Examples

1. The old man has a concave chest.
2. A baseball has a convex surface.

confide

To trust with one's secrets; or, to reveal something in trust.

Example: I asked her to confide in me, and she confided that she was going to elope.

congregate

To come together in a crowd; assemble.

Example: The passers-by congregated around the injured man.

correspond

To be in agreement; or, to be similar in character; or, to exchange letters with another person.

Examples

1. Your version of the accident corresponds with mine.
2. The claws of a cat correspond to the nails of a person.
3. We have been corresponding for 15 years.

PREFIX : DE

The prefix *de* means away; off; or, down, a lessing; or, completely; or, undoing or reversal of an action.

debar

It comes from *de* meaning 'away; off' and the word *bar* meaning 'to shut'. Thus, *debar* means 'to shut out; to exclude'.

Example: He was debarred from club membership because of the scandal.

debark

It is derived from *de* meaning 'away; off' and the old word *bark* meaning 'a ship'. Thus, *debark* means 'to go away from, or off, a ship; to put something off a ship; to go ashore; to unload'.

Example: The ship docked at noon and we debarked immediately.

declare

It is formed from *de* meaning 'completely' and the Latin root *clar* meaning 'to make clear'. Thus *declare* means 'to make completely clear; hence, to say something emphatically; to reveal or prove'.

Examples

1. He declared that he was completely innocent.
2. The judges declared Sam the winner of the race.

dehumidify

It is made up of *de* meaning 'the reversal of an action' and the word *humidify* meaning 'to make humid'. Thus, *dehumidify* means 'to make less humid'.

Example: An air conditioner both cools and dehumidifies the air.

The other words that begin with the prefix *de* are as follows.

decentralise

To recognise into smaller parts away from the centre of something.

Example: If we decentralise, the states will have more autonomy.

decipher

To break down a code or coded message; or, to determine the meaning of something that is hard to read, such as a code or cipher, bad writing, etc.

Example: I can't dicipher what is inscribed on the pillar.

declaim

To speak loudly and in a set, formal way.

Example: A preacher stood declaiming in the town centre.

decline

To bend downward; or, to sink downward; or fail, as in health; or, to turn down or refuse.

Example: He declined to discuss his plans.

decrease

To grow less or smaller; or to take away a part, quantity, rank, etc.

Example: Interest in the game is decreasing.

defend

To turn away injury, danger, etc.; to shield from danger; to protect.

Example: The newspaper defended her against the accusations.

defer

To put off or delay; or, to yield to someone else's opinion.

Example: On technical matters, I defer to the experts.

deflect

To turn something away; to swerve.

Example: The missile deflected from its trajectory.

deform

To distort the form of something; or, to mar the beauty of something or someone.

Example: The accident deformed his limb.

deliver

To set free from something; or, to hand over, to carry and distribute; or, to give or send forth.

Examples

1. May God deliver us from evil.
2. He delivered over his property to his children.
3. Did you deliver my message to your father?

demote

To bring down or lower in rank.

Example: He was demoted from sergeant to corporal.

deplete

To reduce a supply of something, by waste, use, etc.; or, to empty completely.

Example: Our stock of food is greatly depleted.

depopulate

To take away the inhabitants of a place, as by death, war, disaster, etc.

Example: Our country has been depopulated by famine and drought.

depreciate

To lessen the value of; take away value from; or, to become less valuable; lose value.

Examples

1. Don't depreciate my efforts to help.
2. Shares in the company have depreciated.

descend

To go or come down; or, to lower oneself; or, to be derived by heredity.

Examples

1. The balloon descended gradually as the air came out.
2. Be careful not to descend to bad language.
3. She claims to be descended from royalty.

detract

To take away a part of something; to lessen.

Example: This unpleasant incident detracted from our enjoyment

PREFIX EX AND ITS DISGUISES

The prefix *ex* and its disguises *e* or *ef* means out, out of, or from; or, former; or thoroughly or completely.

effervesce

It is formed from *ef* meaning 'out' and the Latin root *fervesc* meaning 'to boil'. Thus *effevesce* means to give off bubbles of gas, as carbonated drinks; or, to be be exhilarated or vivacious.

Examples

1. The soda water is stale and doesn't effervesce.
2. Mary has an effervescent way of speaking.

evade

It derives from *e* meaning 'out' and the Latin root *vad* meaning 'to go'. Thus, *evade* means 'to go or get out of something; hence to avoid or escape'.

Examples

1. The witness tried to evade the lawyer's question.
2. You can circumvent the law, but you can't evade it forever.

exclude

It is made up of *ex* meaning 'out' and the Latin root *clud* meaning 'to shut'. Thus, *exclude* means 'to shut someone or something out, as from a group or place'.

Example: His poor grade in maths excluded him from the honour roll.

excruciate

It comes from *ex* meaning 'completely, thoroughly' and the Latin root *cruciat* meaning 'to torture'. Thus *excruciate* means to inflict extreme pain on someone; to rack with pain.

Example: Walking was excruciatingly painful for the wounded man.

exhume

It stems from *ex* meaning 'out of; from' and the Latin root *hum* meaning 'the ground'. Thus, *exhume* means 'to dig up a corpse or other buried thing'.

Example: The soldier' body was exhumed and shipped home after the war.

The following are other relevant words:

excavate

To hollow or dig out; or, to make a tunnel or hole by digging out the earth.

Examples

1. Indians excavated the cores of fallen trees to make dugout Canoes.
2. Blasting crews will excavate a tunnel under the Alps.

excerpt

A passage picked out from a book, speech, etc., and used or quoted separately.

Example: Several newspapers printed excerpts from the president's memoirs.

excommunicate

To cut someone off from membership in a church.

Example: The Pope excommunicated the priest who was involved in nefarious activities.

exonerate

To free someone from blame; to acquit.

Example: The court completely exonerated the defendant from charges of negligence.

expedite

To speed up the progress of something.

Example: Our new computer has expedited the company's billing operation.

expire

To breathe out one's last breath; to die; or, to come to an end, as a contract or licence.

Examples

1. The old woman expired peacefully in her sleep.
2. I hope you will renew my lease when it expires next year.

PREFIX EXTRA

The prefix *extra* means 'outside of; beyond or outside the range, scope of limits of something'. As a word *extra* is used to mean 'being over and above what is required; additional'.

extraordinary

It is made up of *extra* meaning 'outside of; beyond' and the word *ordinary*. Thus, *extraordinary* means 'being beyond or out of the ordinary; exceptional or remarkable'.

Example: She showed extraordinary presence of mind during the emergency.

extrasensory

It derives from *extra* meaning 'beyond the scope or range of' and the word *sensory* meaning 'having to do with sensation or the sense impulses'. Thus, *extrasensory* means 'beyond the range of normal sense perception; perceived by unknown or unexplained senses beyond the ordinary ones of touch, sight, hearing, etc'.

Example: Do you behave in extrasensory perceptions?

PREFIXES HYPER, HYPO

The prefix *hyper* means 'over; excessive or excessively'.

hyperacidity

This is formed from *hyper* meaning 'excessive' and the word *acidity*. Thus, it means 'an excess of stomach acid'.

Example: Of late she has been suffering from hyperacidity.

hypercorrect

This comes from *hyper* meaning 'excessively' or 'over' and the word *correct,* Thus, it means 'excessively correct or finicky, especially in regard to such things as manners, writing, appearance, speaking, etc'.

Example: A hypercorrect person can be hard to live with.

hypersensitive

This derives from *hyper* meaning 'over' or 'excessively' and the word *sensitive.* Thus, it means 'excessively sensitive or touchy; too easily insulted, angered, disappointed, etc'.

Example: Nancy is so hypersensitive that a tiny rebuke makes her cry.

The prefix *hypo* means 'under or beneath; less than'. Believe it or not, a hypodermic needle and the hypotenus of a triangle are related. Do not confuse *hypo* and *hyper;* they are almost opposite in meaning. *Hyper* means 'over' while *hypo* means 'under'. So, remember the two core vocabulary words beginning with the prefix *hypo—hypodermic, hypotenuse.*

hypodermic

This is formed from *hypo* meaning 'beneath' and the Greek root *derm* meaning 'skin' plus the Latin suffix *ic* meaning 'pertaining to'. Thus, *hypodermic* means 'of or pertaining to the area under the skin'. As a noun, it means 'a syringe for giving under-the skin injections'.

Example: The doctor sterilised the hypodermic needle before giving me the flu shot.

hypotenuse

This comes from *hypo* meaning 'under' and the Greek root *tenus* meaning 'stretching'. Thus, *hypotenuse* means 'the side of a right triangle that stretches under or lies opposite the right angle'.

Example: In geometry we are taught that a hypotenuse is the side opposite the right angle of a right-angled triangle.

hypochondria

Persistent anxiety about one's health.

Example: One who suffers from hypochondria has a morbid anxiety about his health.

hypothesis

An assumption that lies beneath or supports a line of reasoning, and this is therefore accepted as a basis of investigation, argument or further reasoning.

Example: On the hypothesis that the world was round, Columbus hoped to reach the East Indies by sailing westward.

hypothetical

Pertaining to or of the nature of a hypothesis; based on an assumption.

Example: There is no longer anything hypothetical about man's ability to reach the moon.

PREFIXES : OB, OX, OF, OP, OC

The prefix *ob* means 'toward; to; against; completely; over'. As in the case of *ad* and *in,* the spelling of this prefix may change depending on the letter that follows it. Thus, *ob* may be spelled *oc, of,* or *op.* It is often difficult to recognise *ob* as a prefix because of its variants and back of consistent meaning.

obese

This comes from the Latin word meaning 'fat', made up of *ob* meaning 'completely' or 'over' and a verb meaning 'to eat'. Thus, *obese* means 'fat from overeating; very fat'.

Example: She used to be only a bit overweight, but now she is obese.

object

This is formed from *ob* meaning 'against' and the Latin root *jest* meaning 'to throw'. Thus to *object* is 'to throw criticism against something; to oppose something, especially with words'. An *object* is literally 'something thrown in the way'. Hence, the noun *object* means 'something that can be seen or touched' and 'something that is sought for; a purpose or goal'.

Examples

1. The inmates objected to the noise.
2. They spotted an unidentified flying object.
3. The object of the meeting was to elect a new president.

obtrude

This comes from *ob* meaning 'against' or 'toward' and the Latin root *true* meaning 'to thrust'. Thus, *obtrude* mens 'to force or thrust oneself, an opinion, etc., upon another person without being asked'.

Example: Anne loudly obtrudes her beliefs into every conversation.

occupy

This is derived from *oc* (another spelling of *ob*) meaning 'against'and the root *cupy*, which is related to the Latin root *cap* meaning 'to take'. Thus, it means 'to take and hold possession of something, as by force or request' or 'to hold or fill, as an offer or post' or 'to keep oneself busy at doing something'.

Examples

1. Germany occupied France during Word War II.
2. He occupied the major's office for four terms.
3. Can't you find something worthwhile to occupy your mind?

offend

This stems from *of* meaning 'against' and the Latin root *fend* meaning 'to hit'. Thus *offend* literally means 'to hit against or collide with'; hence 'to displease or anger someone' or 'to be disagreeable to the senses', or 'to commit a crime or sin, or to err in some other way'.

Examples

1. I am sorry if I have offended you.
2. The blaring music offended my ears.
3. Nonconformists often offend against the customs of society.

oppress

This is derived from *op* meaning 'against' and the word *press.* Thus, *oppress* means 'to press or lie heavily upon someone, as a burden' or 'to keep in subjugation by harsh use of force or authority'.

Examples

1. The atmosphere of uncertainty oppressed our spirits.
2. They were an oppressed people, enslaved by conquerors.

obfuscate

To confuse or perplex; or, to darken or obscure something.

obligate

To bind or force someone, as with a contract, promise, etc., that necessitates some action, such as the return of a favour or the performance of a duty.

Example: We were obligated to attend the opening ceremony.

oblique

Not following the perpendicular or horizontal; slanting.

Example: He drew an oblique line across the chart.

oblong

Longer in one direction than in another.

Example: She ate an oblong bar of chocolate.

obnoxious

Highly disagreeable; objectionable.

Example: He is the most obnoxious man I know.

obsolete

Out of fashion; no longer used or done.

Example: The horse-drawn plough is not obsolete in most Western countries.

obstetrics

The branch of medicine dealing with pregnancy and childbirth; literally, the branch of medicine that 'stands by' during the process.

Example: She specialises in obstetrics.

obstreperous

Noisy and unruly; literally, making noise 'against, a speaker, someone in authority, etc.

Example: He becomes obstreperous when he's had a few drinks.

obtuse

Not quick in mind or feeling; stupid.

Example: He is being deliberately obtuse.

occult

Pertaining to various magical arts or practices, such as astrology, alchemy and witchcraft, which are 'hidden against' the light of reason.

Example: She indulges in occult practices.

opportune

Timely or favourable; literally, blowing 'toward port', as a ship or a favourable wind.

Example: Your arrival was most opportune.

opprobrium

The state of being reproached or scorned; or, reproach mingled with disdain.

Example : Her behaviour excited opprobrium.

PREFIX : PER

What do a *percolator, perambulator* and a *perjurer* have in common? The prefix *per* means 'through; throughout; by means of; by;' or, 'thoroughly; completely'; or, 'wrongly'.

perambulate

This derives from *per* meaning 'through,' and the word *ambulate* meaning 'to walk'. Thus, the word means 'to walk through or around; to stroll'.

Example: Their vast garden is marvellous for perambulating.

percent

This is a combination of the prefix *per* meaning 'by' and the Latin root *cent* meaning 'the number of parts in every hundred of something'.

Example: He lost nearly ten percent of his accounts.

perfect

This comes from *per* meaning 'thoroughly' and the Latin root fect, meaning 'to make or do'. Thus, it means 'done thoroughly; without fault or blemish; completely suitable'. To *perfect* is 'to make flawless; to improve, refine or complete'.

Examples

1. It is a perfect day for a picnic.
2. Our architect has been perfecting plans for the new house.

perjure

This is formed from *per* meaning 'wrongly' and the Latin root *jur* meaning 'to swear'. Thus, to *perjure* means 'to be guilty of swearing falsely or of giving false testimony while under oath'.

Example: If you falsify your tax return, you are guilty of perjury.

percolate

To pass a liquid or cause a liquid to pass through a filter or strainer; especially, to cause boiling water to filter down through ground coffee.

Example: Let me percolate some coffee.

percussion

The sound produced by means of striking one thing against another; or, musical instruments, such as drums, cymbals, etc.; whose sound is caused in this manner.

Example: He plays the percussion instruments very well.

perdition

Eternal damnation

Example: He hope that the evil person would be damned to perdition.

perfidious

Breaking faith, trust or allegiance, especially through treachery.

Example: We were betrayed by perfidious allies.

permeate

To spread thoroughly through; or, to pass through the pores of something, as of a filter or membrane.

Example: Water has permeated the soil.

pernicious

Having the power to destroy thoroughly; highly injurious; wicked.

Example: Pollution of the water supply reached a level pernicious to the health of the population.

perpendicular

At right angles to or through the horizontal plane; vertical.

Example: The valley ended in a perpendicular rim of granite.

perpetual

Lasting forever

Example: He was irritated by the perpetual complaints.

perplexity

Doubt, confusion or bewilderment

Example: She looked at us in perplexity.

persevere

Continue striving for a purpose in spite of difficulties.

Example: You will need to persevere if you want the business to succeed.

persist

Continue firmly in some course of action; or, be insistent, as in repeating an action.

Examples

1. If you persist, you will annoy them even more.
2. They persisted with the agricultural reforms despite opposition from the farmers

perspective

The effect that distance has upon the appearance of objects, by means of which the eye judges spatial relationships; or, the art or theory of portraying objects on a flat surface so that there is an effect of depth and distance, as in a painting; or, judgement of facts, circumstances, etc., in regard to their proportional importance.

Examples

1. Standing here, you get a perspective of the whole valley.
2. She drew a row of trees receding into the distance to demonstrate the laws of perspective.
3. He sees things in their right perspective.

pertain

To have reference to; relate; or, to belong to something, as a quality, function, etc.

Examples

1. There is a lot of evidence pertaining to this case.
2. He owns the building and the land pertaining to it.

pervade

Spread through every part of something.

Example: The smell of baked apples pervaded the house.

PREFIXES : SUB, SUC, SUF, SUG, SUM, SUP, SUR, SUS

The Latin prefix *sub* means 'under; beneath; below' or 'imperfectly' or 'secretly'.

Like *ad,* the prefix *sub* changes spelling so that its last letter will harmonise with the letter following it. Thus, *sub* may be spelled *suc, suf, sug, sum, sup, sur* or *sus* as in *succumb, suffer, suggest, summon, support, surrogate, suspect.*

subconscious

This is formed from *sub* meaning 'imperfectly' or 'below' and the word *conscious.* Thus *subconscious* means 'not clearly or wholly conscious'. The *subconscious* is 'the part of the mind or mind's activity of which a person is usually not aware; the workings of the mind just below the threshold of consciousness'.

Examples

1. Some people have a subconscious desire for selfdestruction.
2. The psychoanalyst knew that Anita's problem was buried in her subconscious.

submarine

This derives from *sub* meaning 'under' and the word *marine* meaning 'of or having to do with the sea or ships, nautical'. Thus, it means 'existing or operating beneath the surface of the sea'. A *submarine* is designed to operate below the surface of the sea.

Examples

1. Skin divers can study submarine life.
2. An atomic submarine can sail around the world without surfacing.

submit

This comes from *sub* meaning 'under; beneath'; and the Latin root *mit* meaning 'to send or place'. Thus, *submit* means 'to place under or yield to the authority, will or power of another; to surrender' or 'to present for consideration' or 'to present as one's opinion; suggest'.

Examples

1. The English tribes submitted to Caesar's legions.
2. Please submit your report to the board on Tuesday.
3. I submit that we are in error and should change our ways.

suborbital

This stems from *sub* meaning 'less than, almost or imperfectly' and the word *orbital* meaning 'having to do with an orbit'. Thus, *suborbital* means 'not going into orbit; falling short of a complete revolution around the earth or another heavenly body : said of rockets, artificial satellites and spacecraft'.

Example: The missile had a suborbital flight, landing a thousand miles down-range from the launching pad.

subordinate

This is derived from *sub* meaning 'under' and the Latin root *ordain* meaning 'to order' plus the suffix *ate* meaning 'characterised by'. Thus, it means 'belonging to a lower position, class or rank.' A *subordinate* is a person or thing lower in rank or authority than another.

Examples

1. A captain is subordinate to a major.
2. An officer is authorised to give orders to his subordinates.

3. A complex sentence has an independent clause and one or more subordinate clauses.

suborn

This is formed from *sub* meaning 'secretly' and the Latin root *orn* meaning 'to equip'. Thus, to *suborn* means 'to incite someone to an evil or criminal act; especially, to bribe someone to commit perjury or some other criminal act'.

Example: The lawyer was charged with suborning a witness.

subcutaneous

Situated, found or applied beneath the skin.

Example: The doctor gave the child a subcutaneous injection.

subliminal

Perceived below the threshold of consciousness, as certain stimuli, images, etc., of too low an intensity to produce a clear awareness.

Example: Subliminal advertising is sometimes used in television.

subservient

Adapted to promote some higher or more important purpose; useful as a subordinate; servile.

Examples

1. Are priests too subservient to their bishops?
2. People should not be regarded as subservient to the economic system.

subsidiary

A company owned and controlled by another company; or, functioning in a lesser or secondary capacity; auxiliary.

Examples

1. Our company is a subsidiary of the Tata Group of Companies.
2. The question of finance is subsidiary to the question of whether the project will be approved.

subsidy

Financial assistance, especially through government grants, for an individual or enterprise that is thought to be beneficial to the public; literally, money that 'sits under' something in order to support it.

Example: We are planning to increase the level of subsidy to the farmers.

substantiate

Establish as truth by evidence; verify; literally, to 'stand under' something with supporting evidence.

Example: Can you substantiate your accusations against him?

substitute

Put in the place of another; or, a person or thing that takes the place of another.

Examples

1. The understudy was substituted when the leading actor fell ill.
2. The manager was unable to attend but sent his deputy as a substitute.

subterranean

Situated or occurring underground.

Example: The subterranean digging is an ecological disaster.

PREFIX : UN

The prefix *un* means 'not; opposed to; lacking; back' and is often used to indicate the reversal of an action.

The prefix *un* is the last and most important of several negative prefixes that you have learned. What is the difference between *un* and *in*, the two most important of these negative prefixes? Notice that *un* may often indicate a simple lack of something, whereas *in* is more likely to indicate a definite negative, or 'not'. For example, *unapproachable* means 'hard to approach, as a person who is aloof'. In other words, an *unapproachable* person lacks friendliness. *Inapproachable,* if used with precision, means 'not approachable; incapable of being reached'. An isolated place without a road is *inapproachable* by car.

un-American

This comes from *un* meaning 'not opposed to' and the word *American.* Thus, it means 'out of keeping with American character, spirit, ideals, etc'.; or, 'acting against the interests or objectives of the United States' ;or, 'lacking patriotism toward America'.

Examples

1. The conferring of aristocratic titles is un-American.
2. A congressional committee investigates un-American activities on the part of citizens.

unbend

This stems from *un* meaning 'back' indicating the reversal of an action plus the word *bend.* Thus, *unbend* means 'to bend back into place again; straighten' or 'to relax, as after tension, exertion, restraint or familiarity'.

Examples

1. Can you unbend this crooked nail?
2. I unbend after work by watching television.

uncouth

This is formed from *un* meaning 'not' and an older English word that is no longer used: *couth* meaning 'known'. *Uncouth* originally meant 'unknown'. Now, of course, *uncouth* means 'unknowingly'; hence, 'lacking refinement; crude; awkward; boorish'.

Examples

1. It is uncouth to eat peas with a knife.

2. The peasant, though uncouth in manner and appearance, was nevertheless honest and hard-working.

uncivil

Ill-mannered; rude.

Example: It was uncivil of you to say that.

unintelligible

Impossible to understand.

Example: The sick child spoke in an intelligible whisper.

unkempt

Not kept tidy.

Example: The garden looks very unkempt.

unscathed

Not injured or hurt; unharmed

Example: The hostages emerged from their ordeal unscathed.

The word *prefix* itself provides a good example of a prefix and how prefixes work. *Prefix* is made up of the prefix *pre,* meaning 'before', and the root fix, 'to join or fix'. So a prefix is a word element joined on or fixed at the beginning of a word.

1. Latin, and occasionally Greek, prepositions : *ad*jacent, *extra*ordinary, *meta*bolism.
2. Negative prefixes : *un*bending, *in*escapable, *mal*function, *non*committal, *mis*begotten.
3. Prefixes indicating number, degree or amount : *am*bidextrous, *bi*centenary, *semi* circle.
4. Ordinary English words, of whatever origin, whose meanings remain unchanged in compound words : *extra*-special, *over* weight, *under*water, *back*stroke.

The following table shows the language of original, meaning in English and examples of prefixes.

Prefix	*Language of Origin*	*Meaning in Original Language*	*English Examples*
a	Greek	not, without	amoral, historical, asexual
ab, abs, a	Latin	off; away; from	abdicate, abduct, abhor, abort, abnormal, absolve, abstain, abuse
ad	Latin	to, near, at	adapt, adjacent, admire, abbreviate, adopt, accord, affair, aggravate, alleviate, annex, appear, arrive, associate, attend
ambi	Latin	both, around	ambigious, ambitious, ambivalent
an	Greek	not, lacking	anaesthetic, anaemic, anaerobic
ante	Latin	before	antecedent, antedate, antenatal, anteroom, antechamber
anti	Greek	against, oppose to	antibiotic, anticlimax, anticlockwise, antidote, antipathy, antiseptic
bi	Latin	twice, double	bicycle, bigamy, bilateral, bilingual, binoculars, bifocal, binomial, bipartite
cata	Greek	against, opposed to	cataract, catacombs, cataclysm, catarrh
circum	Latin	around, on all sides	circumnavigate, circumlocution, circumspect, circumstance, circumvent

cis	Latin	on this side	cislunar, cisalpine
com	Latin	with, together, thoroughly	combat, combine, compatriot, congregate, concede, coexist, cohere, colleague, collide, confide, correspond
contra counter	Latin	against, opposite	contraband, contradict, contravene, counterattack, counterfeit, counterpart
de	Latin	away, off, less	debar, devise, declare, defend, decipher, dehumidify, decline, demote, descend
deca, dec	Greek	ten	decade, decagon, decalogue, decennial
deci	Latin	a tenth	decibel, decimal, decimate
demi	Latin	a half	demigod, demilune, demitasse
di	Greek	two, twice	decide, diphthong
dia, di	Greek	through, access, apart	diachronic, diagonal, dialysis, dialogue, diaphragm
dis, dif, di	Latin	not, down, less, away	disable, discount, dishonest, disarm, dissolve, dissuade, different, diffuse
epi	Greek	on, over	epicentre, epidermis, epiglothis, epigram
ex, e, ef	Latin	out of, from, former	exclude, exhume, exit, exhale, exhort, effervescent, emit, evade, ex-president
extra	Latin	more, outside	extraordinary, extracurricular, extraterrestrial, extrasensory
for	Old English	completely,	forlorn, forbear, forebid,

fore	Old English	front, before	forehead, foreground, foresight, forecast
hecto, hect	Greek	hundred	hectare, hectogram
hexa, hex	Greek	six	hexapod, hexagram, hexameter
hepta, hept	Greek	seven	heptagon, heptameter
hyper	Greek	over, too much	hyperactive, hypercorrect, hypersensitive, hyperacidity
hypo, hyp	Greek	under, less than, too little	hypodermic, hypochondria, hypothermia, hypothetical, hypotenuse, hypothesis
in, en, em	Latin	in, into	incarnate, income, embrace, enclose, inconsequential, inequitable
in, it, im, ir	Latin	not	inactive, illiterate, impossible, irresistible, imbalance, inarticulate
inter	Latin	among, between, with each other	interbreed, interfere, interject, interlude, intercept, international, intercollegiate, interdependent
intra, intro	Latin	inside, within, inwards	intravenous, intramural, introduce, introverted, intramuscular, introspect, introversion
kilo	Greek	thousand	kilometre, kilogram, kilohertz
mal, male	Latin	bad, evil, wrong	maladroit, malcontent, malediction, malignant
mega	Greek	large, a million	megaphone, megalith, megawatt, megahertz, megadeath, megaton

meta, met	Greek	behind, after, changing	metacarpal, metazoan, metabolism, metamorphosis, metonymy, metalanguage, metaphysics
milli	Latin	thousand	millibar, millisecond, milligram
mis	Latin	badly, wrong	misrepresent, misspell, misanthrope, mistake, misshapen, misread
mono	Latin	one	monomania, monocle, monochrome, monorail, monopoly, monologue
multi	Latin	many, much	multifarious, multiple, multifaceted
non	Latin	not	nonchalant, nonconformist, nonentity, nonsense, nontoxic, noncombatant
ob, oc, of, op	Latin	towards, over against, utterly	obese, object, obtrude, occupy, occult, offend, oppress, opportunity, obtrude, oblong, opprobrium, oppressive
octo, oct	Latin	eight	octopus, octane, octet, octuple
on, out, over	English	on, out, over	onset, onslaught, outermost, outside, overweight, overwrought, oversight
penta, pent	Greek	five	pentacle, pentagon, Pentateuch, pentameter, pentathlon
per	Latin	through, by, utterly, by means of, badly, utterly	perambulator, percolate, perennial, pervade, percussion, perfidious, perfect, persist, perjure, perdition, pernicious, perpendicular, permeate

poly	Greek	much, many	polygamy, polytechnic, polygon, polythene
post	Latin	after, behind	postwar, post meridien, postpone, postscript, postgraduate, posterity
pre	Latin	before	preface, precaution, prefabricated, precept, precipice, premolar
pro	Latin	for, before	proceed, progress, pronoun, produce, profane, profess, provide, project, procure, propaganda, promulgate
quadri, quadr	Latin	four	quadrilateral, quadrangle, quadrille, quadrant, quadruple, quadrillion
re	Latin	back, again utterly	recall, refresh, rebuff, rebel, revise, refrigerate, reinforce, remind, revile
retro	Latin	backwards	retrograde, retrospection
se	Latin	aside, apart, away, without	separate, select, secure, sedition, seduce, segregate, secede
semi	Latin	half	semiconductor, semidetached, semitone
septi, sept	Latin	seven	septuagenarian, Septuagint, septet
sex	Latin	six	sextant, sextile, sextuple, sextet
sub, suc, suf, sug, sus	Latin	under, almost, secodary	submarine, subordinate, suffer, summon, support, sum, surrogate, suspect, sustain, submit, suggest, succumb
super, sur	Latin	above, too	superhuman, supernatural,

		much, on, beyond	superficial, supercilious, surcharge, surcoat, surtax, supervise, superfluous
syn, syl,	Greek sys	together, with	syllable, sympathy, symphony, syntax, synchronise, synopate, syndrome
tetra, tetr	Greek	four	tetrachloride, tetrahedron, tetrameter, tetrasyllable
trans	Latin	across, beyond	translate, transform, transgress, transparent, transmit, transcribe
tri	Greek	three triplicate	trio, triad, triangle,
ultra	Latin	beyond, too much	ultramodern, ultraviolet, untraconservative
under	Old English	beneath, too little	underwear, underwater, underweight, underpay, underrepresented
un	Old English	not, back	unhappy, uncouth, unbend, untie, unsafe, ungrateful, unnatural
uni, un	Latin	one, single	unicycle, unanimous, universe, unity

3

SUFFIXES

Suffixes are less important than roots and prefixes in vocabulary building because they are usually (though not always) added on to a root or word after the primary meaning of the word has been established by the basic root and prefix. In such cases, the suffix serves to indicate the function of the word (that is, its use or part of speech). You should be familiar with suffixes and know how they are used, but you need not learn them as you learned roots and prefixes.

Remember what suffixes are and what they do. They are attached to the ends of words just as prefixes are attached to the beginnings. Suffixes can sometimes change the meaning of a word, but they are primarily used to reveal its function. Suffixes, for example, can indicate the number of a noun by changing the singular form to a plural form. Thus, the suffix *s* added to the word *boy* forms *boys*—the suffix *s* showing that *boy* is plural. For another example, suffixes can indicate the time of a verb by showing whether the action is in the past or the present. Thus, the suffix *ed* added to the verb *talk* forms the past tense *talked*.

To state it another way, the meaning of many suffixes is general. They serve primarily to tell you whether a word is used as an action word (verb), modifier (adjective or adverb), or the name of a person, place or thing (noun); and they serve to distinguish between such things as number and tense.

NOUN SUFFIXES : ACTS, CONDITIONS OR STATES

The following suffixes generally mean :

1. The act, state, quality, means, process, result or condition of doing or being.
2. The beliefs, teaching or system of.
3. Devotion to.

ACITY

audacity

The quality of being audacious; boldness.

Example: He had the audacity to tell me I was too fat.

capacity

The ability to receive, hold or contain; or, mental ability; or, specific character or office.

Examples

1. We have a hall with a seating capacity of 1,000.
2. This book is within the capacity of younger readers.
3. He acted in his capacity as a police officer.

tenacity

The quality of being tenacious; stubbornness; toughness.

Examples

1. The eagle seized its prey in its tenacious grip.
2. She is tenacious in her defence of her rights.

ACY

celibacy

The state of being unmarried.

Example: Catholic priests take a vow of celibacy.

confederacy

The condition of being allied; hence, a union of persons or states for mutual support or action.

Example: The confederacy of all the states has decided to give peace for the world a priority.

fallacy

False or mistaken belief; or, false reasoning or argument.

Examples

1. It is a fallacy to suppose that wealth brings happiness.
2. This is purely a statement based on fallacy.

AL, IAL, EAL

betrayal

The act of betraying or the state of being betrayed.

Example: It is no doubt a dastardly act of betrayal.

denial

The act of denying

Example: He made an official denial that there would be an election soon.

refusal

The acting of refusing.

Example: She has the choice of refusal of an invitation.

ENCE, ANCE, ANCY

influence

The quality or condition of being able to produce effects on others.

Example: The moon has its influence on the tides.

acceptance

The act of accepting or the state of being accepted.

Example: Since we sent out the invitations we have received five acceptances and one refusal.

piquancy

The state or quality of having a pleasantly sharp taste.

Example: The delicate piquancy of the soup goes to the credit of the cook.

ION

audition

The act or scene of hearing; or a hearing, especially a treat hearing of a performer.

Examples

1. I am going to the audition but I don't expect I will get a part.
2. None of the actresses we have auditioned is suitable.

creation

The action of creating; or, anything created, especially by human intelligence or imagination, as an artistic work; or, everything created, the universe.

Examples

1. Economic conditions may be responsible for the creation of social unrest.
2. The chef had produced one of his most spectacular creations, whole roasted duck.
3. All of God's creation are spectacular.

union

The act of uniting or the state of being united; or, the joining of persons, parties, nations, etc., for a mutual purpose.

Examples

1. We would like the union of our party with yours.
2. The newly-wed couple live together in perfect union.

ISM

alcoholism

An abnormal or diseased condition caused by excessive use of alcohol.

Example: This man has been suffering from alcoholism.

heroism

The state or condition of being heroic; bravery.

Example: He was lauded for an act of great heroism.

scepticism

The state or condition of being a sceptic.

Example: All her reports are treated with scepticism.

MENT, MEN

excitement

The state of strong emotion or feeling, especially one caused by something pleasant.

Example: The news caused great excitement.

monument

A memorial erected in memory of a person, event, etc.; or, a tombstone.

Examples

1. A monument was recently erected there to soldiers killed in the war.
2. This is the monument that she built for her husband when he died.

specimen

A person, animal, plant or thing regarded as representative of its class or type; a sample.

Example: There were some fine specimens of rocks and ores in the museum.

acumen

Ability to understand and judge things quickly and clearly; shrewdness.

Example: His business acumen has made him successful.

MONY

matrimony

The state or condition of being married.

Example: The priest united the couple in holy matrimony.

parsimony

The condition of being overly thrifty; stinginess.

Example: She has been practising parsimony and does not believe in donations to the poor.

acrimony

Bitterness of manner or words.

Example: The dispute was settled without acrimony.

OR

error

The condition of being wrong.

Example: The letter was sent to you in error.

SIS, SY, SIA

analysis

An examination of the parts of any complex whole; or, the act of separating a whole into its parts.

Examples

1. Textual analysis identified the author as Shakespeare.
2. English grammar teaches you a lot with the analysis of each sentence.

autopsy

A medical examination of a corpse.

Example: An autopsy report will be useful in analysing the nature of his death.

amnesia

Partial or total loss of memory; the state of having no memory.

Example: This lady has been suffering from amnesia for the past two years.

TUDE

longituade

Literally, the quality of being long (like the lines of longitude on a globe); hence, the distance east or west on the surface of the earth, measure from the prime meridian that runs through Greenwich in England.

Example: The lines of longitude are marked on a map.

multitude

Literally, the condition of being many in numbers; hence, a great number or crowd.

Example: Vast multitudes of birds visit this lake in spring.

TY, ETY, ITY

notoriety

The state of being widely known and generally disapproved of.

Example: His crimes earned him considerable notoriety.

novelty

The quality of being new; or, something new or unusual.

Examples

1. There's a certain novelty value in this approach.
2. A British businessman who can speak a foreign language is still something of a novelty.

superiority

The quality of being superior; excellence.

Example: They won the battle because of their massive superiority in numbers.

URE

aperture

An opening

Examples: The aperture is too narrow for the rod to go in.

curvature

The state of being curved; curved form.

Example: They studied the curvature of the earth's surface.

pressure

The act or result of pressing or weighing down on something.

Example: The pressure of the water caused the wall of the dam to crack.

Y

inquiry

The act of inquiring or seeking for facts or truth; investigation.

Example: In answer to your recent inquiry, the book you mention is not in stock.

perjury

The act of giving false testimony.

Example: They tried to persuade her to commit perjury.

victory

The state or condition of being a victor; the act or result of winning a contest, a war, etc.; success; triumph.

Example: He led the troops to victory.

NOUN SUFFIXES : PEOPLE, PLACES AND THINGS

The following suffixes of nouns all mean:

1. Person or thing that does, practises, or is characterised by or connected with something.

2. A native, citizen or inhabitant of
3. A follower of
4. A place or instrument for

AN, IAN, EAN, ANE

American

A native or inhabitant of America; specifically, an inhabitant or citizen of the United States.

Example: The American decided to settle scores with the German.

crustacean

A type of animal characterised by crustlike shell, as a lobster or crab.

Example: Crabs, lobsters and shrimps are all known as crustaceans.

guardian

One who guards or protects something.

Example: The police are guardians of law and order.

ANT, ENT

inhabitant

A person who lives in or inhabits a specific place.

Example: These are the oldest inhabitants of the island.

resident

A person who resides in a specific house, city, state, etc.

Example: This restaurant is open only to residents.

AR

beggar

A person who begs for his living.

Example: The cheeky beggar asked for my watch too!

scholar

A person connected with or characterised by knowledge or studying.

Example: Dr. Radhakrishnan was a great scholar.

ARY

dictionary

Literally, a book connected with speaking; hence, a reference book, containing the words of a language, arranged alphabetically with meanings, pronunciations, etc.

Example: If you don't know the meaning of this word, look it up in a dictionary.

library

A place for the collection and storage of books.

Example: You can sit in the library and browse through this book.

secretary

Literally, a person who keeps secrets; hence a person employed to handle the records, letters, etc., of a business office or of an individual.

Example: I sometimes think my secretary runs the firm.

ER

baker

A person who bakes bread, cake, etc, for his living.

Example: The baker sold some rolls cheaply.

golfer

A person who plays golf.

Example: The golfer used very few strokes to complete his game.

traveller

A person who travels.

Example: The traveller was exhausted when he returned home.

ICIAN

electrician

A person who designs, installs, operates or repairs electrical wring, equipment, etc.

Example: The elctrician rewired the whole house.

logician

An expert in the use of logic.

Example: You have to accept the logician's argument.

IST

communist

A person who believes in the doctrines of communism.

Example: He is a communist whose ideals are not practicable.

druggist

A person who prepares and deals in medical drugs.

Example: The druggist did not have any of the medicines that were prescribed to her.

genealogist

A specialist in the study of genealogy or family trees.

Example: Ask this genealogist to draw up a diagram of our family's ancestry.

ITE

socialite

A person connected with fashionable social life.

Example: She is a rich socialite moving from one fashionable resort to another.

suburbanite

A person who lives in the suburbs.

Example: The suburbanite travels to the city every Monday to make her purchases for her shop.

OR

agitator

A person or thing that agitates; especially, a person who persists in political or social agitation for change.

Example: The agitator led the women's rally asking for equal rights.

competitor

A person who competes against another.

Example: The firm has better products than its competitors.

donor

A person who gives or donates something

Example: The donor distributed blankets to the needy.

ORY

dormitory

A large room with sleeping accommodations for many persons.

Example: This dormitory can accommodate eight children.

lavatory

A place for washing, as a bathroom or sink.

Example: In British English the toilet in private houses is called the lavatory.

The following suffixes of nouns all mean:

1. The art, science or study of
2. Speech or discourse

ICS, TICS

dramatics

The study or art of drama, the theatre, acting, etc.

Example: She is now into amateur dramatics.

linguistics

The science of language.

Example: She has a doctorate degree in linguistics.

LOGY, LOGUE, OLOGY

biology

The science of life in all its manifestations.

geology

The science that deals with the origin and structure of the earth.

catalogue

A list of names, objects, etc, usually in alphabetical order and often with accompanying descriptions.

dialogue

A conversation between two or more people, actors, groups, etc.

monologue

A long speech by one person.

NOMY

astronomy

The science that deals with heavenly bodies, their motions, distances, etc.

economy

A system for developing and managing material resources; or, careful management of money; thrift.

FAMILIAR SUFFIXES

The following suffixes are widely used, but are not related in meaning as those already discussed.

CRACY

Rule by; government.

democracy

Literally, rule by the people; hence a form of government in which political power is exercised by the people, either directly or through elected representatives.

Example: India is a democracy.

plutocracy

Government by the wealthy; or, class that controls a government by means of its wealth.

Example: This government is a plutocracy in the control of the wealthy elite.

The suffix *cracy* has a related suffix *craft* meaning 'a person who supports a type of government or who belongs to a social class', such as *democrat, plutocrat, aristocrat.*

GRAPH

Writing or drawing; or, an instrument for writing, describing or making sounds.

autograph

Literally, a self-writing; hence, one's own signature; or, to sign something with one's own signature.

Example: I have lots of cricketers' autographs.

telegraph

Literally, distance writing; hence a device using coded impulses that are sent by wire or radio waves as messages; or, to communicate by telegraph.

Example: She greeted the couple on their wedding day by a telegraph.

phonograph

A motor-driven turntable with a pick-up attachment for the playing of phonograph records.

Example: The phonograph is an outdated machine now.

The suffix *graph* has a related suffix *graphy* meaning the art of writing or drawing', as in geography, photography, biography.

METER

A measure; or, an instrument for measuring.

diameter

Literally, the measure through; hence a straight line passing through the centre of a circle and ending at the circumference; or, the length of such a line.

Example: The diameter of this tree-trunk is six feet.

thermometer

An instrument for measuring heat or temperature.

Example: We have a clinical thermometer at home.

The suffix *meter* has a related suffix *metry* meaning 'the art or science of measuring' as in *geometry, trigonometry.*

SCOPE

An instrument for viewing or observing.

microscope

Literally, an instrument for viewing that which is the smallest; hence, an instrument use for magnifying objects too small to be seen, or to be seen in detail, by the naked eye.

Example: She was able to examine bacteria under the microscope in detail.

stethoscope

An instrument used by doctors for listening to the beating of the heart, sounds of beating, etc.

Example: She could feel the faint heartbeats of the baby in the womb with the stethoscope.

telescope

Optical instrument shaped like a tube, with lenses to make distant objects appear larger and nearer.

Example: She could clearly see the stars through the telescope.

SUFFIXES S, ES

Indicates that the noun is in the plural form. It means that there are two or more persons, places or things being spoken of.

Examples

1. The chairs are on the porch.
2. He owns several houses.
3. Foxes have been stealing our chicken.

SUFFIXES : THAT FORM VERBS

The suffixes that follow are added to roots or words in order to form verbs or to indicate the tense of a verb.

ATE, FY, ISH, ISE

These are verb suffixes that mean:

1. To cause to be, become, have, or do.
2. To make
3. To act or act upon
4. To subject to
5. To act in the manner of; practise.

decimate

Literally, to act upon a whole so as to take away a tenth; to select a group by lot and kill one out of every ten; hence, to kill or destroy a large proportion.

Example: Disease has decimated the population.

nominate

Literally, to cause to be named; hence to name or propose as a candidate.

Example: She has been nominated as a candidate for the presidency.

Terminate

To cause to end or stop.

Example: The meeting terminated in disorder.

electrify

Literally, to make electric; hence, to install electricity.

Example: The motor was electrified after repairs.

gratify

Literally, to make pleasing; hence, to please; or, to satisfy or indulge

Examples

1. I was most gratified with the outcome of the meeting.
2. To gratify my curiosity, do tell me what it is.

pacify

Calm or soothe the anger or distress.

Example: He tried to pacify his creditors by repaying part of the money.

admonish

Give a mild but firm warning or scolding to somebody; or, advise or urge seriously.

Examples

1. The teacher admonished the boys for being lazy.
2. She admonished us to seek professional help.

demolish

Pull or knock down a building, etc.; or, eat greedily.

Examples

1. They have demolished the slum distract.
2. She demolished two whole pizzas.

Extinguish

To stop burning; put out; or, end the existence of hope, love, etc.

Examples

1. They tried to extinguish the flames.
2. His behaviour extinguished the last traces of affection she had for him.

christianise

To cause to become Christian.

Example: There is a wide practice here to Christianise the poor people in this area.

terrorise

To subject to terror.

Example: The villagers were terrorised into leaving their homes.

criticise

To point out the faults of somebody or something; or, form and express a judgement on a work of art, literature, etc.

Examples

1. He was criticised by the committee for failing to report the accident.
2. He was teaching the students how to criticise poetry.

S

This indicates that the verb, or action word, is in the present tense. It means that the action is taking place in the present, or that it is habitual or takes place at a regular time. This suffix also indicates that the subject of the verb is the third person singular, that one person or thing—one *he, she* or *it*—is responsible for the action.

Examples

1. She comes to see us every Sunday.
2. He goes to his office every day at nine.
3. The young girl dances well.

4. The late-morning train always arrives on time.
5. It occurs to me that I made a mistake.

ED

This indicates that the verb is in some form of the past tense. It means that the action has taken place and is now either partly or completely finished.

Examples

1. He whisked out of sight as I approached.
2. He has already played in five professional football games.
3. When he was in college, he played cricket.
4. Before he entered college, he had played football in high school.

ING

This indicates that the action word will appear with some form of the verb *to be* and will signify a continuing action. It means that *am, are, is, were, was, has been, have been,* or *had been* is part of the verb form.

Examples

1. I am depending on you.
2. He was driving too fast.
3. We have been trying to work out this sum.

SUFFIXES THAT FORM MODIFIERS

All the following suffixes are added to roots or words in order to form modifiers; they indicate that the new word functions as an adjective or adverb.

AL AND RELATED SUFFIXES

Al (or its variant spelling *ial*), *ar, ary, ic, id, ile, ine, ish, oid* and *ory* are adjective suffixes meaning :

1. Of, pertaining to, of the nature of, like.
2. Having, related to, or serving for.

equal

Of the same size, quality, rank, character, etc.

Example: He speaks Arabic and English with equal ease.

filial

Of or pertaining to a son or daughter.

Example: It is his filial duty to take care of his parents.

manual

Of or pertaining to the hand or hands; done by the hands.

Example: Making small models requires manual skill.

postal

Pertaining to the mails.

Example: Postal applications must be received by the first week of June.

popular

Liked or admired by many people; or, liked, admired and enjoyed by somebody; or, suited to the taste or education level of the general public; or, of or by the people.

Examples

1. Jeans are popular among the young
2. I am not very popular with the boss.
3. We are bringing out novels with popular appeal.
4. Doubtless these are issues of popular concern.

similar

Like something else or one another, but not identical.

Example: We have similar tastes in music.

honorary

Pertaining to an office, title, etc., bestowed as an honour, usually without powers, duties, or salary.

Example: He was awarded an honorary doctorate.

pecuniary

Consisting of or pertaining to money.

Example: She has been working without pecuniary reward.

secondary

Of second rank, grade, influence, etc.; subordinate, subsequent.

Example: Her age is of secondary interest.

academic

Pertaining to an academy college or university; scholarly.

Example: The question is purely academic.

chromatic

Pertaining to colour or colours.

Example: The pictures were chromatic.

despotic

Of or like a despot; tyrannical.

Example: He is surely a despotic headmaster.

gravid

Heavy with child; pregnant.

Example: The gravid woman looks worn out and lethargic.

humid

Having much water vapour, as air.

Example: The humid atmosphere is making me irritable.

lucid

Having light; shining; bright; or, clear; easily understood; or rational; mentally sound.

Examples

1. His style is very lucid.
2. His line of thinking is lauded and hence he has a lucid explanation.

juvenile

Pertaining to the young; youthful.

Example: He is going to play the juvenile lead.

volatile

Literally, flying; hence, changing quickly from one mood to another; or, likely to change sharply or suddenly.

Examples

1. He is a highly volatile personality.
2. A volatile situation now prevails in this city.

bovine

Belonging or pertaining to the family of animals that includes oxen, cows, etc.

Example: The bovine sounds drew us near.

canine

Of or like a dog; or, of the dog family.

Example: The German Shepherd is a canine.

feline

Of or like a cat; of the cat family.

Example: She walked with a feline grace.

boyish

Of or like a boy or boys.

Example: She has boyish good looks.

greenish

Of or like green; somewhat green.

Example: This mould has a greenish-yellow tinge.

ovoid

Like an egg; egg-shaped.

Example: We found large ovoid pebbles on the beach.

spheroid

Similar to a sphere; nearly sphere-shaped.

Example: We found a rather odd spheroid on the seashore.

compulsory

Involving or using compulsion, or being coercive; or, required.

Example: Is English a compulsory subject in your school?

introductory

Serving as an introduction.

Example: They were upset by some introductory remarks by the chairman.

laudatory

Of the nature of praise; complimentary.

Example: You should encourage her with laudatory remarks.

SUFFIX ATE AND RELATED FORMS

Ate, fic, ose, ous, ulent (and its variant spelling *olent*), *ulous* and *y* are adjective suffixes meaning 'full of, like, having, making or causing, given to, or characterised by'.

adequate

Equal to or having what is required.

Example: Our accommodation is hardly adequate.

caudate

Having a tail

Example: The caudate meteor was a spectacular sight.

pinnate

Like a feather; or, having the shape or arrangement of a feather.

Example: The pinnate arrangement of flowers is quite eye-catching.

soporific

Causing or tending to cause sleep.

Example: She was administered a soporific drug.

terrific

Literally, full of or causing terror; hence, extreme, intense or tremendous; or, wonderful, great or splendid.

Example

1. He was driving the car at a terrific speed.
2. The view was terrific.

grandiose

Characterised by grandeur or producing an effect of grandeur; or, potentiously grand.

Example: She had some grandiose plan to start up her own company.

verbose

Wordy

Example: He is a verbose speaker.

glorious

Examples

1. What glorious fun.
2. I would like to die a glorious death.
3. Enjoy this glorious view from here.

joyous

Full of joy; causing joy; joyful.

Example: She suddenly felt a joyous sense of freedom.

opulent

Having or showing great wealth; rich.

Example: He has opulent taste in cars.

redolent

Full of pleasant fragrance; or strongly suggestive.

Examples

1. We entered a room redolent of roses.
2. This is a town redolent of the past.

violent

Coming from or characterised by physical force; or, harsh or severe; or, extreme or intense.

Examples

1. Students were involved in violent clashes with the police.
2. She was in a state of violent shock.
3. The trees were buffeted by violent storms.

credulous

Given to believing on slight evidence; gullible.

Example: They are credulous people who believe what the advertisements say.

populous

Full of people; crowded.

Example: The populous areas near the coast were evacuated.

feathery

Covered with feathers; or, light or airy.

Examples

1. She wore a green, feathery hat.
2. She tried together the feathery snowflakes in her hands.

risky

Characterised by risk; full of risk.

Example: She ventured into a risky undertaking.

ABLE AND RELATED FORMS

Able (and its variant spelling *ible*), *acious, ile* and *ive* are adjective suffixes meaning :

1. Able, able to be, or capable of being.
2. Given to, likely to, or tending to.
3. Characterised by or having the character or quality of

peaceable

Given to keeping the peace; or, powerful or tranquil.

Examples

1. He has a peaceable temperament.
2. Let us adopt some peaceable methods to end this strife.

audible

Capable of being heard.

Example: Her voice was scarcely audible in the classroom.

terrible

Causing great fear or distress; appalling; or, hard to bear; extreme; or, very bad.

Examples

1. There was a terrible murder nearby.
2. The heat was terrible.
3. What a terrible meal!

tenacious

Tending to hold on strongly; hence, holding strongly to opinions, beliefs, etc; or, stubborn.

Examples

1. The mother clasped her child in a tenacious grip.
2. He is tenacious in the observation of his timings.

voracious

Eating with greediness or given to devouring things; or, greedy; or, never satisfied; eager knowledge.

Examples

1. This glutton has a voracious appetite.
2. He is a voracious seeker after truth.

agile

Able to move quickly and easily.

Example: He has an agile mind.

docile

Able to be taught; obedient.

Example: She is a very docile child.

attractive

Tending to attract interest, admiration or affection; or, exerting physical attraction, as a magnet.

Examples

1. Goods are for sale at attractive prices.
2. I don't find her at all attractive.

massive

Having the quality of mass; having great bulk and weight.

Example: The gorilla has a massive forehead.

secretive

Given to secrecy; reticent.

Example: She has a secretive nature.

AN

An (or its variant spellings *ian, ean, ane*) is an adjective suffix meaning:

1. Of, pertaining to, belonging to, or living in
2. Following.

human

Of, belonging to, or characteristic of man.

Example: We must allow for human error.

Confucian

Of or pertaining to Confucius; following the teachings of Confucius.

Example: We cannot understand the Confucian theory.

European

Of, from or pertaining to Europe or its peoples.

Example: The Europeans are a fair race.

urbane

Literally, belonging to the city; hence, having the refinement or elegance of manner associated with city life; suave.

Example: He is an urbane man with a lot of wit.

LESS

Less is an adjective suffix meaning :

1. Lacking or without.
2. Not able to.
3. Not susceptible to or capable of being.

lifeless

Without life; inanimate or dead.

Example: The lifeless bodies of the slaughtered animals lay scattered.

countless

Not capable of being counted; too many to count.

Example: We can see countless stars in the sky.

priceless

Without a price; too valuable to have a price.

Example: They have priceless paintings in their bungalow.

sleepless

Not able to sleep; wakeful.

Example: The baby and mother had a sleepless night.

stainless

Without a stain or spot; or, not susceptible to staining; easy to clean.

Example: The stainless steel sink is easy to clean.

toothless

Without teeth

Example: The baby gave a toothless grin.

ENT

Ent (or its variant spelling *ant*) is an adjective suffix meaning or capable of beingor capable of being 'having the quality of or performing the action of'. In many cases *ent* is equivalent to *ing*.

incumbent

Resting upon one as a moral obligation; obligatory; or, resting, leaning or weighing upon something.

Example: It is incumbent on all users of this equipment to familiarise themselves with the safety procedure.

stringent

Literally, drawing light; hence, compelling adherence to strict requirements; severe.

Example: Use stringent measures to bring him to heel.

dormant

Sleeping or motionless through sleep; or, inactive.

Example: Many plants lie dormant all through winter.

ING

Ing is used to form the present participle of verbs and to form adjectives based on these participles. Among other things, it can mean :

1. now doing the action indicated.

2. for or used for
3. that results in

It is used with these meanings in the following phrases:

a running man

a cooking apple

a winning number

ED

Ed is used to form adjectives based on the past participles of verbs. It means 'one who or that which has been or was'.

Examples

An educated man

An interrupted journey

An overrated book

A scratched table

The suffix *ed* is also used to form adjectives based on nouns. When so used, it means 'one who or that which has, is, or resembles'.

Examples

A four-footed animal

A blue-eyed girl

A stoop-shouldered man

A winged cupid

Dogged determination

An eared seal

ER

Er may be used to form the comparative of both adjectives and adverbs. It means 'more than another or others.'

Examples

colder	higher	smaller	sooner
greater	longer	shorter	later
brighter	greener	duller	sleepier

EST

est may be used to form the superlative of both adjectives and adverbs. It means 'the most; the most of any or of all.'

Examples

coldest	highest	smallest	soonest
greatest	longest	shortest	latest

LY

Ly is a suffix added to words to form modifiers—sometimes forming adjectives from nouns, and sometimes forming adverbs from either nouns or adjectives. It can mean :

1. being or acting as
2. in a certain manner or time.
3. characterised by
4. with respect to

Examples

a friendly man	recently ill
speaking quickly	a perfectly lovely girl
a daily delivery	physically sound
suddenly afraid	mentally unbalanced

4

Combining forms

Combining forms are word elements that can be used to form new words by combining them with words that already exist, other combining forms or various affixes—elements such as *pseudo* in *pseudonym, hypo* in *hypnosis* or *logy* in *zoology.*

Combining forms, unlike many roots and affixes, usually have a single form and a clear, consistent meaning. This is because most are fairly recent in the language, and many are technical and therefore less susceptible to change in day-to-day use.

Most of these combining forms come from Greek or Latin—in some cases from Greek via Latin. Many combining forms turn up also as roots, and some might be seen as prefixes or suffixes.

Most words using combining forms were coined deliberately and consciously, with a view to being 'transparent' in meaning—at least to those with a classical education and the right technical background.

bene, benign

Like its opposite *male* (bad), *bene* (good, well) is simply a Latin adverb used to modify the meanings of words.

A *benediction* is a 'good speaking', particularly a blessing in church.

A *benefactor* is a 'do-gooder', though without negative connotations; it is most often used to mean a 'patron'.

The person who receives the *benevolence* of a benefactor is a *beneficiary.* People who inherit are *beneficiaries* of a will.

Beneficial means 'doing good', in the way that fresh air *benifits* your health.

A related form is *benign,* meant originally 'well-born' or 'noble'. It now turns up in words meaning 'kind, friendly,' such as *benign* and *benignant.* You can compare the change in meaning of the word *gentle,* which also started off meaning 'noble', as in *gentleman* and *of gentle birth.*

logy, ology

The common combining form *ology* (meaning 'study, knowledge') and its derivatives *loger* and *logist,* are ultimately from a Greek word *logos,* 'word, speech'. A related form turns up as the root in words such as *monologue* and *prologue.* An *apology* is a speech in defence.

Knowledge and 'word' are closely related in the Bible. Saint John's Gospel begins as follows : "In the beginning was the word". This is the Greek *logos,* but in Greek philosophical terms it meant 'reason' or 'intelligence'.

Not all *logy* words mean 'the study of something'. Most do—*paleontology, zoology, anthropology*—but others suggest 'speech' or 'expression'. *Phraseology* is a good example.

omni

An all-powerful ruler is *omnipotent.* An all-knowing God is *omniscient.* An animal that eats both meat and plant foods is said to be *omnivorous.*

The modern word *bus* is a contraction of *omnibus,* which in Latin means 'for all, for everybody'. That is, a *bus* is not a private vehicle; everyone may use it.

pan

The Greek equivalent of *omni* is *pan* (all, everywhere). It usually occurs in more technical words than its Latin counterpart. A *panacea* is a 'cure all', a medicene or policy that will solve all problems. A *pandemic* is an extremely wide-ranging epidemic.

Pantheism is the belief that God can be found everywhere and in everything.

Like many combining forms, *pan* can be used almost at will to create new words in the right conditions. It is now generally used with a geographical sense, as in the *pan-African congress* and the *Pan-American Games.*

syn

The Greek *syn,* like the Latin *com,* means 'together'. Like many initial combining forms and prefixes, it may change slightly in form, depending on what letter follows it.

As *syn,* it appears in *synchronise,* 'to make-together-time; *synonym,* a 'together-name'; *synthesis,* a 'bringing together of parts to make a whole'; and *synagogue,* the place where Jews come together to worship. *Syndrome* is a 'running together'. The word refers to a set of symptoms or effects that usually occur together and are characteristic of a disease or condition.

Before an *l* the form changes to *syl.* A *syllable* is a sound 'taken together'.

A *symposium* was originally a 'drinking together' or 'party'. Socrates, according to Plato, used one such party to collect and criticise his 'colleagues' ideas about love. Hence, any serious round-table discussion is called a *symposium.*

In a *symphony* the sounds should match 'together'.

If you show *sympathy* for people you 'feel together' with them, or share their feelings.

Other *syn* words include *syntax, synod, syndicate, synopsis, synthetic, syllogism* and *symmetrical.*

The following chart gives the combining form, language of origin, meaning in English and examples.

Combining Form	*Language of Origin*	*Meaning in English*	*Examples*
aer, aero	Latin	air, atmosphere	aerobic, aerodynamic, aerial, aerofoil, aerosol
agro, agr	Latin	field, farmer	agriculture, agrarian, agrochemical, agrinomy
algia, alg	Greek	pain	neuralgia, analgesic
Anglo	Latin	England	Anglo-Indian Anglo-Saxon, anglophite
Archae	Greek	ancient	archaeology, archaeopteryx
arch, archi	Greek	first, main	archangel, archbishop, archetype, architect
arch, archy	Greek	ruler, form of Government	matriarchy, patriarch, oligarchy, monarch
astro	Latin	star	astronaut, astronomy, astrology
aut, auto	Greek	self	autocrat, autograph, automatic, autonomy
bene, benign	Latin	well, good, kind	benediction, benefactor, beneficial, benefit, benevolent, benign
biblio	Greek	book Bible	bibliography, bibliophile,
bio	Greek	life	biography, biology, biochemist
calc, calci	Latin	chalk, pebble	calcite, calciferous, calculus, calculate

cent	Latin	hundred	centipede, century, centimetre
centr	Latin	middle	centrifuge, centrobaric, centralise
chrom	Greek	colour	chrome, chromatic, chromosome
chron, chrono	Greek	time, age	chronic, chronology, chronometer, synchronic, synchronise, chromosome
cide	Latin	kill, killer	suicide, regicide, insecticide, genocide
cosmo	Greek	world, universe	cosmology, cosmopolitan, cosmic
crat, cracy	Greek	ruler, form of government	democrat, autocrat, bureaucracy, technocracy, aristocracy
crypto	Greek	hidden secret	cryptogram, cryptic, crypto-fascist
dys	Greek	bad	dysentery, dyslexia, dyspeptic
ecto	Greek	external	ectogerm, ectoplasm
ego	Latin	I, self	egotism, egocentric, egotrip
endo	Greek	inside	endogamy, endocrine, endodermis
equ, equi	Latin	equal	equable, equator, equilibrium, equivocal
ethno	Greek	race, people	ethnology, ethnocentric, ethnic
eu	Greek	good	euphonium, euphemism, eugenics
ferro	Latin	iron	ferroconcrete, ferromagnetic
geo	Greek	the Earth	geocentric, geography, geology

gram	Latin	writing	diagram, telegram, aerogram
graph	Greek	draw, write	biography, graphite, graphic
gyro	Greek	circle	gyroscope, gyrocompass
helio	Greek	sun	heliotrope, heliocentric
hetero	Greek	different	heterogeneous, heterosexual
haem, him	Greek	blood	haemoglobin, haematite, haemorrhoids, haemophilia, haemorrhage
homo	Latin	same, equal	homogeneous, homosexuality
hydro	Greek	water	hydroelectric, hydrofoils, hydraulic, dehydrate
hypno hypn	Greek	sleep	hypnosis, hypnotic, hypnotherapy
itis	Greek	inflammation	appendicitis, meningitis
iso	Greek	equal, alike	isobar, isotherm, isomer
lacto, lact	Latin	milk	lactoprotein, lactose, lactic
lign	Latin	wood	lignite, lignocellulose, ligneous
litho	Greek	stone	lithograph, lithosphere, monolith
logy, ology	Greek	study, science	zoology, phonology, phraseology
macro,	Greek	large, long	macrocosm, macrobiotics, macr macroscopic
mal, male	Latin	bad, badly	maladroit, maladministration, malignant, malediction, malevolent
meso	Greek	middle	mesomorphic, Mesopotamia, Mesozoic

meteor	Greek	weather, atmosphere	meteorology, meteorite, meteoric
meter	Greek	measuring device	barometer, metre, metricate, nanometer
micro	Greek	small	microscope, micrometer, microdot
mid	Old English	middle	midnight, midriff, mid-winter, mid-summer
monger	Old English	seller, dealer	fishmonger, gossipmonger, costermonger
morph	Old English	shape	morphology, amorphous
neo	Greek	new	neologism, neo-Nazi, Neolithic
neuro, neur	Greek	nerve	neurosurgeon, neuralgia, neuron
omni	Latin	all, utterly	omnipotent, omnivorous, omnibus
ortho	Greek	straight, correct	orthopaedics, orthography, orthodox
osis	Greek	process, disease	metamorphosis, osmosis, tuberculosis, neurosis
palaeo, paleo	Greek	old, ancient	Palaeontology, palaeography, paleolithic
pan	Greek	everywhere all	panacea, pantheism, pan-African
pathy, path	Greek	disease, feeling	antipathy, psychopath, sympathy, pathological, pathology
petro, petr	Latin	stone	petrify, petroleum, petrology
phobia,	Greek	fear,	claustrophobic, agoraphobe,

phobe, phobic		aversion	xenophobia
phon, phono	Greek	sound	photograph, phonetics, telephone, stereophonic, anglophone
photo	Greek	light	photograph, photoelectric
pseudo, pseud	Greek	false	pseudonym, pseudo-intellectual
stat	Greek	regulator	thermostat, rheostat
stereo	Greek	solid, 3D	stereobate, stereophonic, stereoscopic
syn, sym syl	Greek	together, same	synchronise, synagogue, syllable, symphony, system, sympathy
tele, tel	Greek	far, long distance	telephone, telecommunications, telepathy
thermo	Greek	heat	thermometer, thermodynamics
topo	Greek	place	topography, toponymn
trope, tropic	Greek	direction, version, change	heliotrope, phototropic, troposphere, tropic
zoo	Greek	animal	zoological, zoomorphic

5

THE ANIMAL KINGDOM

Did you know that you are a viviparous mammalian biped? The following words describe some of the major types of animals that inhabit the earth, characterising them according to the class they belong to, their physical make-up, their habits, or the way they bring forth young.

amphibian

1. *In popular use:* an animal that can or seems to live both in the water and on land, as a crococide, seal, etc.
2. *In scientific use:* a class of animal that lives in the water at one stage of its life and on land at another, as the land-living frog, which starts life as a water-living tadpole.

acquatic

Living in or near water, as fish, whales, ducks, etc.

arboreal

Living in trees, as most birds, monkeys, etc.

biped

An animal having only two feet, as man, apes and birds.

carnivorous

Describing an animal that feeds chiefly or exclusively on meat, as dogs, wolves, lions, tigers, etc.

diurnal

More active during the day than at night, as man, apes, birds, grazing animals, etc.

herbivorous

Describing an animal that feeds mainly on vegetable matter; plant eating.

mammalian

Describing an animal that suckles its young with milk from breasts.

marsupial

A member of an order of whose females nourish and protect their newborn in a pouch in the abdomen, as kangaroos and opossums.

monotreme

A member of the lowest order of mammals whose females lay and hatch eggs, as the duck-billed platypus.

nocturnal

More active during the night than in the daytime, as bats, certain insects, some cats, etc.

oviparous

Belonging to a class of animals whose females lay and hatch eggs, as birds, most fishes and reptiles.

pachyderm

Any of certain thick-skinned, non-ruminant, hoofed animals, as the elephants, rhinoceros and hippopotamus.

prehensile

Capable of or adapted for grasping or holding, as the hands or paws of man and some apes, monkeys, bears, opossums, etc., and the tails of certain monkeys.

6

PEOPLE WHO BECAME WORDS

For better or for worse, people have given their names to many common words. Sometimes the reasons are scientific or practical, and sometimes not so serious. Given below are words that grew from personal names, some famous and some forgotten.

Adonis

A beautiful youth. Adonis, the young man in Greek mythology was adored by Aphrodite, the goddess of love and beauty.

August

The eighth month of the year. Named after Augustus Caesar.

bloomers

Women's loose, baggy trousers drawn close at the ankles and worn under a short skirt, or a woman's undergarment resembling these. Bloomers were named after Mrs. Amelia Jenks Bloomer (1818-94), an American champion of women's rights.

bobby

A British policeman. This word, the familiar form of Robert, came into use after Sir Robert Peel set up the police system in London early in the nineteenth century. These London policemen were first called 'Bobby's men' and later just 'bobbies'.

bowdlerise

To censor any kind of writing in a prudish manner. The word immortalises an English editor, Dr. Thomas Bowdler, who produced a 'family' edition of the works of Shakespeare by removing every word or passage that offended the sense of propriety.

boycott

To refuse, as a group, to buy from or have any dealings with a person or organisation, in order to reduce prices or bring about some change; also, an instance of this. The word comes from C.C. Boycott, a British army officer and landlord's agent in Ireland in the nineteenth century, who was the first victim of boycotting because of his unpopularity among tenants from whom he collected rents.

Caliban

A brutish person, typically deformed both in appearance and in personality. The word comes from the character in Shakespeare's *The Tempest.*

Casanova

A playboy noted for his amorous adventures, a lady-killer. After the Italian adventurer and womaniser, Giovanni Giacomo Casanova.

Cassandra

A prophet of doom, particularly one whose warnings are unheeded. After the Trojan princess in Greek mythology, who was endowed with the gift of prophecy but destined never to be believed.

chauvinism

Militant glorification of one's country; vain patriotism. After Nicholas Chauvin, a devoted soldier and overzealous supporter of Napoleon Bonaparte.

dahlia

A flower that takes its name from Anders Dahl, the eighteenth century Swedish botanist who developed it.

Draconian

Rigorous, harsh or cruel. After *Draco,* chief magistrate of Athens, who introduced a harsh penal code in 621 BC

epicure

A person given to discriminating luxury; a fastidious devotee of good food and drink; a gourmet. After the Greek philosopher Epicurus, who taught that peace of mind, cultural interests, and a discriminating temperance in sensual pleasure lead to the good life.

Galahad

A chivalrous and gallant man. After the knight of King Arthur's Round Table, celebrated for his pure and noble character.

gerrymander

To set the boundaries of voting districts in such a way that one political party will have an unfair advantage in elections. After Elbridge Gerry, US Politician + (*sala*) *mander*, from the salamander-like shape of an electoral district formed in 1812 while Gerry was governor of Massachusetts.

guillotine

A machine used for beheading a person by means of a heavy knife that drops between two posts. It was named after J.J. Guillotin, a French physician, who developed it. It was used especially on victims of the French Revolution.

Jezebel

A shamelessly immoral or scheming woman. After Jezebel, wife of Ahab, the Old Testament king of Israel; she promoted idolatry and the murder of prophets.

July

The seventh month of the year. Literally, it means 'the month of Julius' because it was inserted into the calendar by Julius Caesar.

lynch

To execute summarily, usually by hanging, without a proper trial. Probably after Captain William Lynch, an eighteenth century Virginian planter and Justice of the Peace.

Macadamise

To pave a road with layers of small or cracked stones, usually with a tar or asphalt binder. The word comes from J.L. McAdam, a Scottish engineer who invented the method.

machiavellian

Cunning, crafty, seizing opportunities. After Niccolo Machiavelli (1469-1527), a Florentine statesman; in his book, *The Prince,* he described how a determined ruler could gain and keep political power regardless of morality.

mansard

A roof that is flat on the top and has sharp, vertical slopes at the edges. Named after a French architect, Francois Mansard, who popularised this style in the seventeenth century.

Martha

A worrier, a person constantly preoccupied with everyday chores and cares, often at the expense of things of higher significance. After the sister of Lazarus and Mary, who buried herself with household tasks while Mary listened to Jesus.

martinet

A person, such as a teacher, army officer, etc., who believes in and enforces strict discipline. The word comes from Gen. Jean Martinet, a French drill-master in the seventeenth century who invented a new system of military drill.

Matahari

A female spy, typically very beautiful or glamorous. After the Dutch spy, Margaretha Geertruida Zelle (1876-1917), who worked as a dancer in Paris under the stage name *Mata Hari* and spied for both France and Germany in the First World War. She was finally executed by the French.

maudlin

Excessively and tearfully emotional or sentimental. From Mary Magdalen, who is often depicted with her eyes swollen from weeping.

mausoleum

A large, stately tomb. From King Mausolus of Caria, whose large tomb, erected by Queen Artemisia at Halicarnassus in Asia Minor about 350 BC, was one of the Seven Wonders of the World.

maverick

An unbranded or orphaned animal as a calf; an unorthodox person. From Samuel A. Maverick, a nineteenth-century Texas lawyer who refused to brand his cattle.

mesmerism

The process or practice of inducing a hypnotic state; or the state itself. After Dr Franz Anton Mesmer (1734-1815), a German physician. who popularised the practice.

Micawber

An incurable optimist, a poor person who remains doggedly hopeful despite all his misfortunes. After Wilkins Micawber in Dickens's novel *David Copperfield,* who keeps insisting that 'something will turn up'.

Midas

A person with the gift of making money. Hence, the Midas touch: the gift of making money. After the legendary king of Phrygia to whom was given the power of turning to gold all he touched.

Munchhausen

A person who tells tall stories. After the fictionalised hero, Baron Munchhausen, of a book of fantastic adventures, published in 1785, by the German traveller Rudolph Raspe.

namby-pamby

Weekly sentimental or childishly simple. From 'Namby-Pamby', a poem of about 1715, written by Henry Carey to satirise the sentimental verses of his fellow-poet, Ambroze Philips. Namby is a baby-talk nickname for Ambrose.

nicotine

A poisonous, oily alkaloid found in tobacco leaves. Named after Jean Nicot, the French courtier who introduced tobacco into France from Portugal in the sixteenth century.

pasteurise

To destroy germs and check fermentation in milk, beer, wine, etc., by the use of high temperatures. The word comes from Louis Pasteur, the famous nineteenth-century French chemist and the father of modern bacteriology.

quisling

A person, a traitor, who betrays his country by helping an invader. Named after a Norwegian traitor, Vidkun Quisling, who collaborated with the Nazis and became a Nazi party leader during World War II.

Rasputin

A faith healer, particularly one who gains a sinister hold over those who fall under his influence. After the monk Grigori Rasputin (1872-1916), who treated the haemophiliac son of the last Russian Tsar, and exerted an extraordinary influence over the Russian Imperial family as a whole.

Robespierre

A person fanatically and cold-bloodedly dedicated to a cause. After the French leader Maximilien Robespierre (1758-94), chief architect of the Reign of Terror and famous for his austere and incorruptible character.

shrapnel

A kind of shell containing pieces of sharp metal that shoot out in all directions when the charge is exploded. Named after its inventor, Harry Shrapnel (1761-1842), an English artillery officer.

sideburns

Short side whiskers reaching from the hairline to below the ears. The words comes from *burnsides*—side whiskers and moustache, worn with the chin clean-shaven—named after the Civil War Union general, A.E. Burnside.

silhouette

A portrait made by tracing the outline of a profile, head or figure, and filling it in with black. After Etienne de Silhouette (1709-1767), a French author and politician, possibly because he decorated his residence with outline portraits.

Svengali

A person with mysterious powers to make others do his will. After the villainous musician in George du Maurier's novel *Trilby*, who powerfully influences and manipulates Trilby, the heroine.

thespian

An actor or actress also, relating to drama or the theatre. After Thespis, a poet of the sixth century BC, traditionally regarded as the father of Greek tragedy.

tartuffe

A religious hypocrite. After the title character of Mohaire's comic play *Tartuffe*.

Walter Mitty

An impractical daydreamer, a person who escapes his humdrum life by indulging in vivid daydreams of romantic adventures and personal triumphs. After the central character in James Thurber's story. 'The Secret Life of Walter Mitty' (1939).

7

PLACES WHICH BECAME WORDS

A place that produces some special item or idea may also produce the name for it. *Champagne* is so called because it comes from the Champagne district of France. More indirectly, *jeans* comes from Genoa, the *spaniel* from Spain, and *copper* from Cypress.

The following are words, with their meanings, and the places that gave birth to the names.

afghan

A coverlet that is limited or crocheted from soft woollen yarn. Such coverlets originally came from Afghanistan.

Argyle

A plaid design of diamond-shaped blocks of solid colour overlaid by a contrasting plaid. The design is the tartan of the clan Campbell of Argyle, a country of western Scotland.

arras

A tapestry, usually hanging on a wall, French Arras, cloth of Arras, a city in northern France.

artesian

Relating to deep wells, from which water flows under pressure.

French *artesian*, well of Artois, a region in northern France where such wells were first drilled.

bedlam

A scene of wild uproar. The word is a corruption of Bethlehem, and comes from the name of a former insane asylum, the hospital of Mary of Bethlehem in London, England.

bologna

A seasoned sasuage of mixed meats. It was named after Bologna, Italy.

calico

A cotton cloth printed in figured pattern of bright colours. This word comes from Calicut cloth, named for the city where it was originally made, Calicut, India.

cantaloupe

A variety of muskmelon. It was named after an Italian castle, Cantalupo, where this melon was first successfully grown in Europe.

damask

A silk or linen fabric with a woven pattern. Named after Damascus, Syria, where it was first made.

denim

A tough cotton cloth, often dyed blue, as used for jeans and overalls, French *de Mimes*, serge cloth from Nimes, a city in Southern France.

eau de cologne

A toilet water consisting of alcohol scented with aromatic oils. It was named for the city of Cologne in West Germany.

ermine

A stoat whose coat turns white in winter; also, its valuable white fur. From Mediaeval Latin *Armenius*, mouse of *Armenia*.

frankfurter

A smoked sausage made of beef or beef and pork, or one of these served on a long bun. This American dish comes from Frankfurt, Germany.

frieze

Decorated panel running horizontally along a wall, often just below the ceiling; also, the decorated band at the top of a classical column. From Latin *Phrygium,* work of Phrygia (today part of Turkey), famous for its gold embroidery.

hessian

A coarse fabric like sacking, made of jute; as in *bales packed in hessian.* After Hesse, now a state in Germany, where it was originally produced.

homburg

A man's felt hat, with an upturned brim and a dented crown. After Homburg, a small town in Germany, where it was first manufactured.

kersey

A woollen fabric, woven with diagonal ribs or lines, often used for coats. Probably after the Suffolk village of Kersey.

limousine

A large motor car, often having three rows of seats. French limousine, originally meaning a cloak, worn by shepherds in Limousin, a region in west central France; the name was then applied to early motor cars because the projecting roof on some of them apparently resembled a cloak in shape.

magenta

A deep red colour; also, a red dye. After Magenta, a town in northern Italy; the bloodshed in a famous battle there, in 1859, gave rise to the name of the newly discovered red dye.

majolica

A type of decorated and enamelled pottery, glazed in rich colours, widely made in sixteenth-century Italy, and initited in the nineteenth century. From Majolica, a mediaeval name for the Balearic island of Mallorca (or Majorca), where the style originated.

meander

To follow a winding route, as a river might; also, to wander about aimlessly. After the winding river Maiandros or Meander in Phrygia—today the river Menderes in Turkey.

parchment

A kind of stiff paper, formerly made of goatskin or sheepskin. Partly after Pergamum, an ancient Greek city in Asia Minor, where animal skins were treated—today Bargema in Turkey.

ritzy

Luxurious; very fancy or fashionable (a slang word). After the elegant Ritz hotels, especially the Ritz-Carton Hotel in New York.

sardonic

A mocking; scornful; as in *She declined the offer with a sardonic smile.* Partly after Latin *Sardonica,* herb of Sardinia, a poisonous plant so bitter that one tends to pull a face on tasting it.

shallot

An edible bulb similar to the onion. From Latin *Ascalonia,* onion of Ascalon, a seaport in ancient Palestine—today Ashkelon in Israel.

spa

A health resort having mineral spring. After Spa, a resort in Belgium noted for its mineral waters.

spartan

Austere; rigorous; as in a *Spartan childhood at boarding school.* After

Sparta, an ancient Greek city-state famous for its harsh military discipline and cultural rigidity.

sybaritic

Relating to luxurious living; as in *indulging in sybaritic vices.* After Sybaris, a very wealthy and notoriously loose-living ancient Greek colony in southern Italy.

turquoise

An opaque blue-green gemstone; also, a blue-green colour. From old French *turquoise,* stone of Turkey or Turkestan, where it was first mined.

8

Pairs that Snare

Some words sound and look nearly alike, but have different meanings. Words that look or sound alike are often called *homonyms,* and we are so used to such pairs that most of them do not trouble us. Thus, few people confuse *ate* and *eight; know* and *no; pore* and *pour; wait* and *weight;* or *bark* (of a dog) and *bark* (of a tree). Where problems of usage do occur is with pairs of words that are both similar enough and different enough to be confused with one another.

Someone has described such usage problems as 'pairs that snare'—and we are using that phrase for the title of this chapter. The word pairs or groups listed in alphabetical order are truly traps for the unwary. A good speaker or writer must distinguish between these sound-alike, look-alike words. Learn exactly what each word means in the following list, and how to spell and use it exactly. Given below are homonyms with their meanings and examples.

ACCEDE, EXCEED

accede

To consent or agree; or, to come into office.

Examples

1. I will accede to your plan.
2. The prince acceded to the throne.

exceed

To surpass; to go beyond the limit of.

Examples

1. For safety's sake, don't exceed the speed limit.
2. This year's profits exceeded last years.

ACCEPT, EXCEPT

Accept

To take something offered.

Example: I accept your invitation.

except

To exclude or leave out; with the exception of.

Examples

1. When I say I like fruit, I except plums.
2. No one is going except Kenneth.

ACCESS, EXCESS

access

A way of getting to something or someone.

Example: Few people have access to the FBI's files.

excess

Surplus; overabundance

Examples

1. This year there is an excess of eggs on the market.
2. The bill was in excess of Rs. 1,000.

ADAPT, ADOPT

adapt

To adjust; to fit or make fit.

Example: Eskimos learn how to adapt to the cold.

adopt

To take as one's own.

Examples

1. We are going to adopt a child.
2. The club adopted a new set of rules.

ADVICE, ADVISE

advice

Rhymes with *ice* and has a hissing sound. It is a noun and means 'counsel, suggestion or information'.

Example: Consider Mary's advice carefully before you take it.

advise

Rhymes with *eyes* and has a buzzing sound. It is a verb and means 'to give advice to; counsel'.

Example: I advise you to try to stay in school.

AFFECT, EFFECT

affect

To influence

Example: Government decisions affect the future of us all.

effect

To bring about a result; to produce or accomplish something,' or, a result or consequence.

Examples

1. The doctor will try to effect a cure.
2. His medicine had a good effect on me.

AISLE, ISLE

aisle

A passageway.

Example: The bride and groom walked up the aisle.

Isle

They vacationed on the Isle of Man.

ALL READY, ALREADY

all ready

Means that all or everything is ready or prepared.

Example: The house is all ready for us to move in.

already

Previously, earlier; by this time.

Example: We had already left when the accident happened.

ALL TOGETHER, ALTOGETHER

All together

All or everything that is together in the same place or at the same time.

Example: The guests arrived all together.

altogether

Completely; absolutely.

Example: You are altogether wrong.

ALLUSION, ILLUSION

allusion

A reference or mention

Example

The preacher made an allusion to Homer.

illusion

A false impression; something that seems to be something else or that actually does not exist.

Example: The white walls create the illusion that the room is very large.

ALTAR, ALTER

altar

A platform or raised area, as in a church.

Example: The bride and groom stood before the altar.

alter

Change

Example: The tailor altered the bride's dress.

ANECDOTE, ANTIDOTE

anecdote

A short narrative.

Example: He told an anecdote about his childhood.

antidote

Something that counteracts a poison, disease or bad mood.

Example: What is the antidote for arsenic?

ANGEL, ANGLE

angel

A heavenly being; an extremely beautiful or sweet person.

Example: Hark! The herald angels sing.

angle

A geometric figure formed by two straight lines meeting; a projecting corner; a point of view.

Examples

1. The dog disappeared around an angle of the house.
2. The problem must be studied from all angles.

ASSURE, ENSURE, INSURE

assure

Guarantee; state with confidence.

Example: I assure you that his intentions are good.

ensure

Make certain

Example: These measures will ensure the success of our programme.

insure

To guard against loss or harm.

Example: When you mail this package, insure it.

BAITED, BATED

baited

Containing or holding bait, as a trap of a fish-hook.

Example: My poor dog fell into a baited trap.

bated

Held in.

Example: He waited with bated breath.

BESIDE, BESIDES

beside

At the side of; next to.

Example: He lives in a house beside a huge tree.

besides

In addition to; moreover.

Example: It was snowing; besides, it was below zero.

BLOND, BLONDE

blond

A fair-haired person of either sex; or, a golden colour.

Examples

1. The brother and sister are both blonds.
2. Is the table made of blond wood?

blonde

A blond woman or girl.

Example: Many gentlemen prefer blondes.

BRAKE, BREAK

brake

A device that stops or slows down; or, to reduce the speed of.

Examples

1. The car needs new brakes.
2. The boy braked his bicycle to a stop.

break

To smash; or, an opening.

Examples

1. Don't break the window.
2. There is a break in the clouds.

BREATH, BREATHE, BREADTH

breath

Air from or in the lungs.

Example: Asthmatics are often short of breath.

breadth

Inhale and exhale.

Example: Now that the pollution has cleared, you can breath easily.

breadth

Width; the opposite of length.

Example: What are the length and breadth of this chest?

BRIDAL, BRIDLE

bridal

Of or pertaining to a bride.

Example: Her bridal gown was trimmed with lace.

bridle

Headgear attached to the reins to control a horse; or, of or pertaining to horseback riding; or, to draw in the chin through anger, pride, etc.

Examples

1. Put on the bridle and saddle on the mare.
2. We galloped along the bridle path.
3. Our probing questions made him bridle.

BRUNET, BRUNETTE

brunet

A dark-haired man, or the colour of his hair.

Example: My brother is a brunet.

brunette

A dark-haired girl or woman, or the colour of her hair.

The blonde's sister is a brunette.

CANON, CANNON

canon

A rule or law, especially of religious faith; sacred books.

Example: This canon has been enacted by the church council.

cannon

A large gun, often mounted on wheels.

Example: An old cannon stood at the entrance to the fort.

CANVAS, CANVASS

canvas

A sturdy cloth.

Example: The tent is made of canvas.

Canvass

To solicit votes, sales, opinions, etc., especially by going from house to house.

Example: We canvassed the neighbourhood selling magazines.

CEDE, SEDE

cede

Grant, give up something.

Example: Germany ceded territory to Poland in 1945.

seed

That from which something is grown.

Example: We planted watermelon seeds.

CENSER, CENSOR, CENSURE

censer

A vessel for burning incense, as in religious ceremonies.

Example: The priest swung the censer.

censor

A person who examines books, plays, letters, etc., to prohibit what seems objectionable; or, to prohibit, suppress or remove allegedly objectionable material.

Examples

1. The censor cut a scene from the movie.
2. Every dictator censors the newspapers in his country.
3. The military censor examined mail from the war zone.

censure

Reprimand, blame or denounce.

Example: The principal censured the students for their rude behaviour.

CHAFE, CHAFF

chafe

Irritate or make sore by rubbing.

Example: The tight collar chafed my neck.

chaff

Tease or make fun of; or; or, the husks of grain.

Examples

1. It is impolite to chaff a stranger.
2. Separate the wheat from the chaff.

CHORD, CORD

chord

A combination of three or more musical tones; or, a string or strings of a guitar, violin, etc.; or, an emotional response; or, in geometry, a straight line intersecting a curve or arc.

Examples

1. The opening chords of the symphony were very long.
2. The chords of the guitar are made of nylon.
3. His sad words struck a responsive chord in her, and she began to cry.
4. Chord AB connects the ends of the arc AB of circle C.

cord

A string, rope, etc., used to tie something; or, an insulated electric wire with a plug at one end; or, a cubic measure for fuel wood; or, a rib, as in fabric; or, a cordlike part of the body.

Examples

1. Tie the box with this cord.
2. The toaster needs a new electric cord.
3. We bought two cords of firewood.

4. Wear your cord jacket.
5. Shouting strains the vocal cords.

CITE, SIGHT, SITE

cite

Quote or refer to

Example: I would like to quote a passage from Shakespeare's *The Merchant of Venice.*

sight

Something seen; or, vision; or, an aiming device; or, to see.

Examples

1. The Red Fort is one of the sights of New Delhi.
2. He lost the sight in one eye.
3. The sight of that gun needs adjusting.
4. We sighted land on Tuesday.

site

A place where something is located.

Example: The site of the Taj Mahal is Agra.

CLENCH, CLINCH

clench

Close tightly

Example: The angry boy clenched his first.

clinch

Secure firmly by bending down a protruding point, as of a nail or staple; or, make sure of; or, the act of grasping.

Examples

1. Sam clinched the nails of the bookcase he was building.
2. He tried hard to clinch the sale.
3. The fighter went into a clinch.

COARSE, COURSE

coarse

Composed of large particles; or, vulgar.

Examples

1. Use coarse-grained sugar, not powdered sugar.
2. He made a coarse remark.

course

Direction; or, passage or duration of time; or, progress; or, a series of actions or events making up a unit; or, ground passed over; or, a series of classes, or a curriculum of studies; or, a portion of a meal; or, a line of conduct.

Examples

1. Our course was due north.
2. In the course of the week, he completed the job.
3. The disease must run its course.
4. My uncle is taking a course of treatments for arthritis.
5. John liked walking on the golf course.
6. He took a chemistry course in high school.
7. The main course was veal and potatoes.
8. You are following a wise course.

COMPLEMENT, COMPLIMENT

complement

Complete or perfect; or, that which completes; or, a complete number or amount.

1. A red scrarf complemented her outfit.
2. A good dessert is always a complement to a fine meal.
3. The ship had a full complement of crewmen.

compliment

An expression of praise or admiration; or, to express praise or admiration.

Examples

1. He heaped compliments on her cooking.
2. I would like to complement you on your cooking.

COMPLEMENTARY, COMPLIMENTARY

complementary

Serving to complete; or, referring to one of two colours that when mixed produce a third colour.

Examples

1. Husbands and wives often make complementary remarks—one finishes what the other begins to say.
2. Blue and yellow are complementary colours.

complimentary

Conveying or using praise; or, given free.

Examples

1. To tell a woman she looks haggard is hardly a complimentary remark.
2. The new shop handed out complimentary packs of chocolates.

CONSUL, COUNCIL, COUNSEL

consul

A foreign-based government official below the rank of ambassador.

Example: Is there a Swedish consul in India?

council

A group of people organised to deliberate or rule; or, a meeting.

Examples

1. The city council meets once a month.
2. The Council of Trent was held in Italy in the sixteenth century.

counsel

To advise; or, advice; or a lawyer or adviser.

Examples

1. Will you listen to my counsel?
2. His guardian counselled him well.
3. Is the plaintiff's counsel in court?

CORE, CORPS

core

The centre, especially of fruit.

Example: She threw an apple core into the wastebasket.

corps

An organised unit of people.

Example: He joined the Peace Corps.

CURRANT, CURRENT

currant

A small black or red berry.

Example: Try adding currants in your cake mix while baking it.

current

Continuous outward flowing, as of water or electricity; or, belonging to the present.

Example

1. Tides and currents affect ships.
2. Phil's electric razor works only on alternate current.
3. Current events sometimes scare me.

DAIRY, DIARY

dairy

A farm or barn where milk cows are kept; or, a place where milk and milk products are prepared and sold.

Examples

1. The Sharmas run a dairy farm.
2. We bought milk and ice-cream at the local dairy.

diary

A daily record or journal.

Example: I keep a diary of daily happenings.

DECENT, DESCENT, DISSENT

decent

Suitable; respectable

Examples

1. Please wear a decent suit to the party.
2. She was a decent woman of modest means.

descent

Act of coming down.

Example: Our descent from the kill was painfully slow.

dissent

To differ; disagree; or, difference of opinion; disagreement.

Examples

1. Three justices dissented from the court's decision.
2. Justice Bhagavati filed many suitable dissents in the Supreme Court.

DESERT, DESSERT

desert

An arid region; or, to abandon or forsake.

Examples

1. Lawrence rode a camel across the desert.
2. He intended to desert his wife and child.

dessert

A sweet course at the end of a meal.

Example: Strawberry souffle is my favourite dessert.

DEVICE, DEVISE

device

A contrivance, as a tool or aid.

Example: He invented a device for cracking ice.

devise

To invent or construct.

Example: He devised a new way to make bread rise.

DIE, DYE

die

To perish; or, to stop or diminish

Examples

1. The grapes will die on the vine.
2. The sound died away.

dye

To colour by a chemical process; or, the colouring matter used.

Examples

1. She dyed her head red.
2. The dye in this shirt is running and fading.

DUAL, DUEL

dual

Double

Example: My sports car has a dual carburettor.

duel

A prearranged combat between two people, usually with swords or pistols; or, any contest between two people.

Examples

1. He killed his enemy in a duel.
2. Chess is a duel of wits.

EMIGRANT, IMMIGRANT

emigrant

A person who leaves one country to move to another.

Example: The Italian emigrants got on the boat at Naples.

immigrant

A person who enters one country from another.

Example: The immigrants to America got off the boat in New York.

EMINENT, IMMINENT

eminent

Well-known, distinguished; highly respected.

Example: Watson is an eminent biologist.

imminent

About to happen; impending.

Example: He predicted that an earthquake was imminent.

ENVELOP, ENVELOPE

envelop

To wrap or enclose.

Example: Fog often envelops the local airport.

envelope

A paper wrapper, as for a letter.

Example: He addressed and stamped the envelope.

FAINT, FEINT

faint

Timid, feeble; or, to lose consciousness briefly.

Examples

1. Alice felt faint with hunger.
2. Victorian ladies often fainted at the sight of a mouse.

feint

A mock attack or blow; to make a mock attack in order to divert attention from a real one.

Example: He feinted with his left and hit me with his right.

FARTHER, FURTHER

farther

At a greater distance.

Example: I can see farther than you can.

further

More; in addition to

Example: I have nothing further to report.

FIANCE', FIANCE'E

fiance'

A man who is engaged to be married.

Example: He is Mary's fiance'.

fiance'e

A woman who is engaged to be married.

Example: Mary is his fiance'e.

FLAUNT, FLOUT

flaunt

To make a gaudy display; to show off something.

Example: Some hostesses like to flaunt their wealth.

flout

To defy

Example: He flouts all rules, but he will get caught some day.

FORMALLY, FORMERLY

formally

In a formal way.

Example: Have you two been formally introduced?

formerly

Some time ago; previously.

Example: West Virginia was formerly part of Virginia.

FOUL, FOWL

foul

Disgusting; evil; or, out-of-bounds; or, something that is out-of-bounds or against the rules.

Examples

1. A foul smell arose from the swamp.
2. "Foul ball!" shouted the umpire.
3. The boxer was disqualified for committing a foul.

fowl

A chicken, duck, turkey or pheasant.

Example: He has never eaten any kind of fowl.

IDLE, IDOL, IDYLL

idle

Not active

Example: The plant was idle during the strike.

Idol

An object or image of a god; a person who is greatly admired.

Examples

1. Pagan people often set up idols to worship.
2. Tom Cruise is every boy's idol.

idyll

A poem or prose work that concentrates on simple, pastoral scenes; or, any very attractive, simple scene or event.

Examples

1. Tennyson's *Idylls of the King* is a very moving poem.
2. Our summer in Nantucket was an idyll.

INGENIOUS, INGENUOUS

ingenious

Clever; imaginative.

Example: Ingenious minds dream up ingenious plans.

ingenuous

Naive; frank and open.

Example: Gloria has an ingenuous way of believing everything she hears.

LATER, LATTER

later

More late; after some time.

Examples

1. It is later than you think.
2. My father got home later than I did.

latter

The second of two.

Example: I like both apples and pears but prefer the latter.

LEAD; LED

lead

A metal (rhyming with dead); or, to be first to conduct (rhymes with need).

Examples

1. He picked up a section of the lead pipe.
2. He wants to lead an orchestra later.

Led (rhymes with red)

The past tense of the verb *lead.*

Example: He led in the race initially, but eventually lost.

LOOSE, LOSE

loose

Not tight; untied or free.

Example

1. This shirt collar is too loose.
2. Let the dog loose.

lose

To misplace; to suffer the loss of; or, to be beaten.

Examples

1. Did you lose your wrist watch yesterday?
2. You will lose interest in studies if you keep watching movies so often.

MINER, MINOR

miner

A person who works in the mine.

Example: He began as a coal miner

minor

A person who is under age; or, of little importance.

Examples

1. In this state, you are a minor until the age of 18 years.
2. Even minor inconveniences infuriate her.

MORAL, MORALE

moral

Adhering to the laws of God and man; or, a point or lesson.

Examples

1. Gandhiji was a moral and just person.
2. The moral of the story is "Beware of flattery".

morale

A state of mind in terms of confidence and courage.

Example: The morale of our troops is high.

NAVAL, NAVEL

naval

Referring to a navy or ships.

Example: Naval battles helped win World War II.

navel

The sunken indentation in the abdomen, or any similar indentation.

Examples

1. I think a swimming suit should cover the navel.
2. She ate a navel orange for lunch.

PASSED, PAST

passed

Past tense of the verb *pass*, meaning, to have gone by, got by or moved through; or, to have handed something to someone.

Examples

1. He passed the exam easily.

2. We passed the gate without seeing it.
3. She passed the salt to him.

past

Having already happened; time gone by

Examples

1. This past week was very warm.
2. The past is over, so don't worry about it.

PEACE, PIECE

peace

Freedom from war or disturbance.

Example: Let us pray for peace in our time.

piece

A part or portion.

Example: I will have a piece of the cake.

PEDAL, PEDDLE

pedal

A foot-operated lever.

Example: A pedal of the bicycle fell off.

peddle

To sell at retail; to hawk.

Example: Where do you plan to peddle these items?

PERSONAL, PERSONNEL

personal

Of, for, or belonging to a particular person.

Example: A man's letters are his personal property.

personnel

The people employed on a job; or, of or having to do with workers.

Examples

1. The company takes good care of its personnel.
2. Apply for a job in the company's personnel office.

PRECEDE, PROCEED

precede

To go in advance of; to come first.

Examples

1. The usher preceded us down the aisle.
2. A precedes B in the alphabet.

proceed

To go on or go forward.

Example: If there are no further questions, I will proceed with the lecture.

PRESCRIBE, PROSCRIBE

prescribe

To recommend or set down a rule to be followed.

Example: The doctor prescribed absolute rest for the patient.

proscribe

To ban something, as by decree.

Example: Cannibalism is proscribed in many societies.

PRINCIPAL, PRINCIPLE

principal

Major; or, a person who takes a leading part; or, capital as opposed to interest.

Examples

1. Carelessness is a principal cause of highway accidents.
2. The principal of the school attended our concert.
3. The principal was Rs. 1,000 and the interest 5% a year.

principle

A general rule or truth, as in ethics or morality.

Example: It is not the money but the principle of the thing that matters.

QUIET, QUITE

quiet

Calm; still; silent.

Example: This quiet, moonlit night fits my mood.

quite

Entirely; or; really; or, noticeably.

Examples

1. That is, I assure you, quite true.
2. Mary felt quite ill during dinner.

RAIN, REIN, REIGN

rain

Liquid precipitation.

Example: The forecast is for rain today.

rein

A device used to guide a horse.

Example: Adjust the saddle and reins.

reign

To rule, as a sovereign; or, the rule of a sovereign.

Examples

1. Cromwell reigned over England like a king.
2. It happened in the reign of Hitler.

RAISE, RAZE

raise

To lift something; or, to grow or breed something.

Examples

1. Raise your right hand.
2. He raises chickens.

raze

To demolish.

Example: The wreckers began to raze the building.

RESPECTABLY, RESPECTFULLY, RESPECTIVELY

respectably

In a worthy or proper manner.

Example: The man seemed poor, but he was respectably dressed.

respectfully

In a respectful or polite way.

Example: Children should speak respectfully to their elders.

respectively

In a specified order.

Example: The German, the British and the American drank beer, whisky and wine, respectively.

STATIONARY, STATIONERY

stationary

In a fixed position; standing still.

Example: The population of Denmark remained stationary for a century.

Stationery

Writing paper and related materials.

Example

He bought a notebook at the stationery shop.

STRAIGHT, STRAIT

straight

Not curved or crooked.

Example: A straight line is the shortest distance between two connecting points.

strait

A narrow passage of water connecting two larger bodies of water; or, a restricted or distressing situation.

Examples

1. We passed the Strait of Malacca.
2. That family next door is in dire financial straits.

SUIT, SUITE

suit

A coat with matching trousers or skirt; or, a series of playing cards; or, a proceeding in a law court; or, the courting of a woman.

Examples

1. Grandfather still wears a blue suit every Sunday.
2. If hearts are trumps, why didn't you lead another suit?
3. Robert's lawyer argued his suit eloquently.
4. After the briefest of suits, Juliet said yes to Romeo.

suite

A set of rooms, of matching furniture, or related musical compositions, etc.

Examples

1. They reserved the bridal suite at the Ritz.
2. My cousin has a new living-room suite.
3. Everybody loves Tchaikovsky's 'Nutcracker Suite'.

THAN, THEN

than

When compared with; except; but

Examples

1. I am taller than you.
2. I refer to none other than our president.

then

At that time; in that case; for that reason.

Examples

1. Life was easy in the 1800's; there were no cars then.
2. If you won't go, then I will, and then you will be sorry.

THEIR, THERE

their

The possessive form of *they*.

Example: It is their house.

there

At that place.

Example: Put the box over there.

threw

The past tense of *throw.*

Example: She threw another blanket on her sleeping child.

through

From one side or one end to the other.

Example: Let us walk all the way through the woods.

thorough

Complete

Example: She gave the room a thorough cleaning.

TO, TOO, TWO

to

Forward; in the direction of.

Example: He drove from Delhi to Agra.

too

Also; or, more often.

Examples

1. I, too, can solve hard problems.
2. This candy is too sweet.

two

The number after one.

Example: Two is the only even prime number.

VAIN, VANE, VEIN

vain

Conceited; or, useless.

Examples

1. That model is an unusually vain girl.
2. Several vain attempts to find a job discouraged Charles.

vane

A direction pointer

Example: The weekend farmers bought a new weather vane for the barn.

vein

A blood vessel.

Example: The lumberman cut a vein, not an artery.

WAIST, WASTE

waist

The narrow part of the body above the hips, or the corresponding part of a garment.

Example: She has a very slender waist.

waste

Needless consumption or destruction; or, refuse.

Examples

1. I think golf is a waste of time.
2. The waste from the factory polluted the river.

WEATHER, WHETHER

weather

Day-to-day climate.

Example: What is the weather forecast for today?

whether

If it be the case that; in case.

Example: I shall go whether or not you do.

WHOSE, WHO'S

whose

The possessive of the pronoun *who.*

Example

Whose book is this?

who's

The contraction of *who is.*

Example: Who's going with me?

9

THE LURE OF THE EAST

Throughout history, Europeans have been fascinated by the mystery and beauty of the East. They have traded in its goods, and later brought much of its territory within their colonial empires. The English language reflects these centuries of close contacts. Even a word as everyday as *tank*, for example, comes from Hindi. The words *orange* and *spinach* go back, through old French, to Arabic, and then to Persia.

The following are the words from the Orient, with their meanings, an account of in each case of how the word arrived in the English language.

alcove

A recessed area in a wall or room.

From Arabic *al-qubbah,* literally, the vault.

antimacassar

A cloth covering on a chair, especially to protect against dirt.

Anti-(protection against)+*macassar* (a hair-oil), after *Makassar,* today called Ujung Pandang, a city in Indonesia which exported the ingredients for hair-oil.

arsenal

A stock of weapons; also a place here they are stored, made, or repaired.

From Arabic *dar-as-sina'ah,* literally, a house of manufacture.

attar

A perfume made from petals, as in *attar* of roses.

Persian *attar,* perfumed.

azure

Sky-blue.

From Arabic *al-lazaward,* the gemstone lapis lazuli.

calico

A cotton cloth—plain and white in Britain, coarse and dyed in the United States.

After *Calicut,* today Kozhikode, a seaport in south-western India, where it was produced and shipped.

cipher

A numeral; also, the number zero; an insignificant person; a system of secret writing, and so on.

From Arabic *sifr,* zero; related to *decipher.*

drab

To beat with a stick.

Arabic *daraba,* to beat.

garble

To confuse; to garble a message or report is to confuse it so badly that it becomes incomprehensible.

From Arabic *ghirbal,* a sieve.

gingham

A cotton fabric, woven from coloured yarns in stripes, checks or plaids.

From Malay *ginggang,* striped cloth.

hookah

An Eastern smoking pipe, with a tube for passing the smoke through water to cool it.

From Arabic *huqqah,* a small box.

kedgeree

In England, a hot dish of fish, rice and eggs; in India, a dish of lentils, rice, eggs and onions.

From Hindi *khichri.*

kowtow

To be over-respectful, to behave in a seriously submissive way, as in *kowtowed to her in all her unreasonable demands.*

Originally, a Chinese greeting involving a deep bow until one's forehead touches the ground. Mandarin Chinese, *ke,* to bump + *tou*, the head.

nabob

A wealthy and important man; originally, a ruler in India in the days of the Mughal Empire.

Portuguese *nababo,* from Urdu *nawwab* a ruler.

pagoda

A temple or tower, usually ornate and many-storeyed, in the Far East.

Probably from Persian *butkada : but,* an idol + *kada,* a temple.

pariah

An outcast; originally, a member of a low caste of drummers in South India.

Tamil *Paraiyan,* a drummer.

pundit

An expert or authority in a particular field. Originally, a Hindu scholar.

Hindi *pandit,* a learned man.

purdah

The seclusion of women; originally, a curtain used in the East to conceal women from men, particularly in India.

Hindi *purdah,* a screen, from Persian.

shanghai

To kidnap a man, often by drugging him, to serve on shipboard; press-gang.

After *Shanghai,* the great Chinese seaport; sailing ships heading there were often crewed by such kidnap-victims.

10

NEW WORDS FROM OLD BOOKS

The stories of the *Bible* and the myths of ancient Greece and Rome have contributed much to Western culture. They have also added to our stock of words. The word *money,* for example, is derived ultimately from the name of a Roman goddess, Juno Moneta, whose temple was used as a mint in ancient Rome.

The following words have meanings, with brief accounts of each word's mythological or biblical origins.

aeolian

Produced by the wind or relating to the wind, as in *aeolian erosion.* An *aeolian harp*—or wind harp—is a sound box with strings that produce musical sounds when the wind passes over them.

After *Aeolus,* the Greek god of the winds.

bacchanalian

Given to drunken revelry, riotously drunken. Also a drunken reveller.

After Bacchus, the Roman god of grape-growing wine and pleasure.

chimerical

Imaginary, unreal, wildly fanciful.

After *Khimaira*, literally, she goat, a fire-eating monster in Greek mythology, usually with a lion's head, a goat's body, and a serpent's tail.

gorgon

A frighteningly ugly woman.

After any of three monstrous sisters in Greek mythology who had live snakes for hair, and turned anyone who looked at them to stone.

iridescent

Producing a shimmering, rainbow-like array of colours.

After *Iris*, Greek goddess of the rainbow.

Janus-faced

Hypocritica, two-faced.

After *Janus*, the Roman god of gates and doorways, usually represented with two faces looking in opposite directions.

jeremiad

A prolonged and mournful complaint, lament, warning or criticism.

After Jeremiah, the old Testament prophet, and reputed author of lamentations on the moral and spiritual decline of the kingdom of Judah and its approaching downfalls at the hands of the Babylonians.

jeroboam

A very large wine-bottle or goblet, in Britain usually containing the equivalent of six normal bottles.

After Jeroboam I, the Old Testament king of Israel, and a mighty man of valour.

jovial

Merry, jolly, convivial; originally, born under the influence of the planet Jupiter, considered by astrologers to be the source of happiness.

From Latin *jovialis,* of or relating to Jupiter.

Junoesque

Having a stately bearing and imposing beauty.

After Juno, the principal Roman goddess, patroness of marriage.

martial

Of; relating to or characteristic of war or the military life.

After *Mars,* the Roman god of war.

mutational

Relating to the morning, early. After *Matuta,* the Roman Goddess of dawn.

mentor

A wise adviser, a faithful teacher or guide ultimately.

After *Mentor,* Odysseus's faithful friend and counsellor in Homer's *Odessey,* who became the teacher and guardian of Odysseus's son Telemachus; probably the direct source of the word is a later version of the same character, in the moral romance *Telemaque* by the French philosopher Francois Fenelon.

mercurial

Volatile, changeable in character, as in *mercurial temperament;* sprightly, lively, shrewd.

After *Mercury,* the Roman god of commerce, travel and thievery, and also the messenger of the other Gods.

narcissism

Self-love and admiration.

After *Narcissus,* in Ovid's *Metamorphoses,* who fell in love with his own reflection in a spring.

nemesis

A person or thing that inflicts revenge or retribution, an avenger; also, the execution or workings of retributive justice.

Greek, literally, retribution; also the goddess of retribution; from *nemein,* to distribute what is due.

odyssey

A long adventurous and wandering journey.

After the ancient Greek epic poem *Odyssey* by Homer, describing the ten year's wandering of Odysseus on his way home to Ithaca after the fall of Troy.

paean

A passionate expression or song of praise or thanksgiving. From Greek *paian,* a song or chant addressed to Apollo, from his title *Paian* as physician to the gods.

palladium

A safeguard; anything believed to censure the safety of a nation, institution or the like, as in *treat by jury, the palladium of Britain's liberties.*

From Greek *Palladion,* the statue of the goddess *Pallas* Athena in Troy, on which the safety of the city was held to depend.

philistine

A coarse, boorish person, lacking in culture and often actively hostile towards it. After the *Philistines,* the people of ancient Philistia in old Testament times, for long the chief enemies and oppressors of the Austerities; adapted from German Philister, a Philistine, a name once applied by German university students to towns people who were not members of their university.

saturnine

Having a taciturn, gloomy character, showing the characteristics of one born under the astrological sign Saturn. After *Saturn,* the Roman god of sowing or seed.

11

GIFTS FROM LITERATURE

If someone has a *Jekyll-and-Hyde* personality, he or she tends to undergo sudden and perhaps frightening changes in mood or behaviour.

The expression comes from the character in Robert Louis Stevenson's novel of 1886. There are many other words and phrases in English similarly derived from the names of literary characters and places, some of which are given below.

diddle

Cheat or swindle, probably after Jeremy *Diddler,* a swindler in James Kennedy's play *Raising the Wind* (1803).

euphuism

An affectedly high-flown style of writing or speaking.

After *Euphues,* a character in two works by John Lyly, a contemporary of Shakespeare's, who popularised an elaborate and high-falutin style of writing; the name derives in turn from Greek *euphues,* shapely, well-grown.

Falstaffian

Fat, jolly, loose-living and boastful. After Sir John *Falstaff,* the lazy and immoral but fun-loving knight who appears in Shakespeare's *Henry IV* plays and *The Merry Wives of Windsor.*

gamp

A large, shabby umbrella. After Mrs. Sahar *Gamp,* a character in Dickens's novel *Martin Chuzzlewit,* who owns a large, baggy umbrella.

gargantuan

Enormous, gigantic, huge. After King *Gargantua,* the huge and energetic hero of satirical books by the sixteenth-century French humourist, Francois Rabelais.

grundyism

Prudish or narrow-minded moral criticism of books, behaviour or the like. After Mrs. *Grundy,* a stern old-fashioned character in Thomas Morton's play *Speed the Plough.*

Lilliputian

A very small person or being; also, tiny or puny.

After the tiny inhabitants of Lilliput, an imaginary island in Jonathan Swift's satire *Gulliver's Travels.*

lotus-eater

A person who neglects work and lives only for pleasure.

After a North African people in Homer's *Odyssey* who lived on the fruit of the lotus in a state of drugged indolence.

malapropism

A misapplication of a word by confusing it with one that sounds similar, as in "He is the very *pineapple* of politeness" (instead of *pinnacle).*

After Mrs *Malaprop,* a character in Richard Brinsley Sheridan's comic play *The Rivals,* who habitually makes mistakes; the name derives in turn from the French *mal a' propose,* literally, not to the purpose.

Pecksniffian

Constantly talking, often hypocritically, about kindness and other virtues.

After the self-righteous Şeth Pecksniff in Dicken's novel *Martin Chuzzlewit.*

quixotic

Romantically idealistic, ignoring practical realities, caught up in the romance of noble ideals and deeds.

After Don *Quixote,* the hero of surgical romances by the Spanish writer Miguel de Cervantes.

serendipity

The faculty of making lucky discoveries by chance.

After the lucky heroes of the *Three Princes of Serendipity,* a traditional tale set in Sri Lanka (at one time known as Serendip); the term was coined in 1754 by the writer Horace Walpole.

utopian

Very worthy but impractical or unrealistic, as in *a utopian proposal for reform.* After *Utopia,* the imaginary island representing a perfect society, described in Sir Thomas Moore's book of the same name.

yahoo

A coarse or brutish person.

After the ape-like *yahoos,* representing humanity at its most brutish in Swifts *Gulliver's Travels.*

12

CONFUSED WORDS

Here begins an alphabetical list of 'confused words'. These confused words are usage problems because their meanings are related in some way. Thus, *allude* and *refer, flotsam* and *jetsam,* and *imply* and *infer* do not sound or look alike, yet many people confuse them because their meanings or uses are related.

Many of these pairs are among the most interesting in our language. Once you are truly at home with them, you can have fun helping to settle the debates of those of your friends who are still unsure about the distinctions between these words.

AGGRAVATE, IRRITATE

aggravate

To make worse.

Example: His discomfort was aggravated by a toothache.

irritate

To annoy or vex.

Example: Kitty's constant nagging irritated her husband.

ALLUDE, REFER

Allude

To mention directly or in passing.

Example: He alluded to his past job but didn't go into the details.

refer

To mention directly or in detail.

Example: He referred literally to his most recent clash with the foreman.

ALUMNUS, ALUMNI, ALUMNA, ALUMNAE

alumnus

A male graduate.

Example: Eisenhower was an alumnus of West Point.

alumni

Graduates, whether male, or both male and female.

Example: My son and my daughter are both alumni of Delhi University.

alumna

A female graduate.

Example: She is an alumna of Lady Shriram College.

alumnae

The plural of *alumna.*

Example: Both my daughters are alumnae of Women's Christian College.

AMONG, BETWEEN

among

Refers to three or more things having some sort of loose relationship to one another; or, in the midst of; amid.

Example

1. He found the textbook he wanted among the many others on the shelf.
2. Steven relaxes only when he is among his friends.

between

Refers to two related things, or to more than two when each is being compared to or related to each of the others.

Examples

1. Susan sat down between her brother and his friend.
2. There was a bond between the members that held our whole group together.

AMOUNT, NUMBER

amount

Quantity in bulk or mass.

Examples

1. He spent a small amount of money.
2. He ate a large amount of mashed potatoes.

number

Quantity in terms of separate items or units.

Examples

1. The tenants filed a number of complaints against the landlord.
2. George owns a small number of books.

ANXIOUS, EAGER

anxious

Distressed with worry.

Example: The mother was anxious about her child's health.

eager

Happily expectant.

Example: The mother was eager to visit her married daughter.

APT, LIKELY, LIABLE

apt

Inclined to as a matter of course; usually expected to; or, quick to learn.

Examples

1. It is apt to be hot in summer.
2. Henry is an apt student of the practical sciences.

likely

Probable; expected but not as a matter of course.

Example: The weather report says it is likely to be hot tomorrow.

liable

Responsible for the consequences; or, in danger of experiencing something disagreeable.

Examples

1. A husband is liable for his wife's debts.
2. If you play tennis at high noon, you are liable to get a heat stroke.

BECAUSE OF, DUE TO

Because of

By reason of; on account of

Example: We lost the match because of my errors.

due to

Same meaning as 'because of', but is preferably used only when you can substitute *caused by.*

Example: My absence was due to illness.

CAN, MAY

can

To be able to

Example: John, who is only thirteen, can drive a car.

may

To have permission to

Example: Because of his youth, Frank may not drive a car even though he knows how.

COMPARE, CONTRAST

compare

One compares *like* things, things that are of the same class or kind.

Example: How does your new car compare with the old one?

contrast

One contrasts *unlike* things, things that are of different kinds or classes.

Example: Contrast a horse and buggy with a modern car.

CONNOTATION, DENOTATION

connotation

What a word suggests or implies.

Example: The word 'snake' has unpleasant connotations for most people.

denotation

The specific meaning of a word.

Example: The denotation of 'snake' is simply this: a legless reptile with a long, thin body.

CONTEMPTIBLE, CONTEMPTUOUS

contemptible

Deserving of contempt.

Example: Hitler was a contemptible person.

contemptuous

Churchill was always contemptuous of Hitler.

CONTINUAL, CONTINUOUS

continual

Over and over again; regular but interrupted.

Example: We had a continual series of hot spells last summer.

continuous

Nonstop; constant and not interrupted.

Example: Many plants and animals thrive in the continuous jungle heat.

CREDIBLE, CREDITABLE, CREDULOUS

credible

Believable

Example: His story, though unusual, is credible.

creditable

Praiseworthy; to one's credit.

Example: His grades in school are very creditable.

credulous

Gullible; too much inclined to believe.

Example: Only a credulous person would fall for that old trick.

DISINTERESTED, UNINTERESTED

disinterested

Impartial; unbiased.

Example: An umpire must be an entirely disinterested but keep observer.

uninterested

Not interested; uncaring

Example: I am uninterested in any TV programme that lacks comedy.

EGOIST, EGOTIST

egoist

A self-centred, selfish person.

Example: An egoist lives for his own pleasure.

egotist

A person who boasts about himself.

Example: She is such an egotist that she talks about herself all the time.

ELDER, ELDEST

elder

Careful writers once used *elder* and *eldest* for *older* and *oldest* in comparing ages, as a brothers and sisters. However, most people now use *older* and *oldest* exclusively, except in the use of 'elder statesman'.

explicit

Specifically said or written.

Example: When we have discussed your debt, you made me the explicit promise of repayment by January.

implicit

Implied or understood but not directly stated.

Example: Though we never discussed it openly, there was an implicit understanding between us that you would return the money.

FEWER, LESS

fewer

Applies to number, to separate items, units, parts, or portions that can be counted. It tells how many.

Example: She has fewer books than Rahul.

less

Applies to amount or quantity of non-separable things.

Example: Apples cost less money than lemons.

FLOTSAM, JETSAM

flotsam

A ship's goods or parts found floating in the water.

jetsam

A ship's goods or parts thrown overboard (jettisoned) in order to lighten a ship that is in danger of sinking.

The literal distinction between these words is important only to marine lawyers and nautical writers. The rather hackneyed expression *flotsam and jetsam,* which derives from the literal meanings, generally refers to any worthless trifles found 'floating' around on sea or land.

HANGED, HUNG

hanged

Put to death by hanging.

Example: The spy was hanged at noon.

hung

Suspended or cause to be suspended from a wall, ceiling, etc.

Example: We hung our reproduction of the 'Mona Lisa' above the sideboard.

HISTORIC, HISTORICAL

historic

Famous in history.

Example: The formation of the United Nations was a historic occasion.

historical

Concerned with history.

Example: I read historical books and often visit our local historical society.

IF, WHETHER

if

Introduces a cause-and-effect relationship, or suggests doubt.

Examples

1. If it rains, we won't go to the races.
2. I wonder if it is raining in St. Louis.

whether

Introduces an indirect question or an alternative.

Examples

1. He asked whether we would go if it rained.
2. We will go whether or not it rains.

IMMORAL, AMORAL

immoral

Violating morality; sinful.

Example: It is immoral to steal another man's wife.

amoral

Not subject to moral judgment; lacking a knowledge of right and wrong.

Example: Cats are amoral; they can't be censured for killing birds.

IMPLY, INFER

imply

To suggest or hint.

Example: He implied that my friend had stolen a necklace.

infer

To conclude or derive from.

Example: From what he said, I inferred that he believed John had stolen a necklace.

IN, INTO

in

Indicates location, position or situation.

Examples

1. I walked in the park for an hour.
2. She held a child in her arms.
3. The doctor is in his clinic.

into

Indicates direction or motion to or toward a location or situation.

Examples

1. I walked into the park at 9.30.
2. The doctor just went into his clinic.

INCREDIBLE, INCREDULOUS

incredible

Hard to believe.

Example: It is incredible that you could have made such a mistake!

incredulous

Sceptical; hard to convince.

Example: I was credulous when I heard that you—you, of all people—had made such a mistake.

LEARN, TEACH

learn

To acquire knowledge or skills.

Example: Students learn.

teach

To import knowledge or skills.

Example: Teachers teach.

LEAVE, LET

leave

To go away from; to depart.

Example: When does the next plane leave for London?

let

To permit

Example: Will you let me go to London?

LIE, LAY

lie

To recline

Example: Lie down on the couch.

lay

To put something down.

Example: Lay the plate on the table.

The confusion occurs because the past tense of *lie* is *lay.*

The present tense of *lay* is *lie:* Lie down on the couch.

The past tense of *lay* is *laid:* He laid the plate on the table.

LUXURIOUS, LUXURIANT

luxurious

Characterised by luxury.

Example: The Governor lives in a luxurious house.

Luxuriant

Growing lushly; abundant.

Example: She has a luxuriant head of red hair.

MAJORITY, PLURALITY

majority

More than half.

Example: He won the election by a clear majority.

plurality

More than any other, but not more than half the total.

Example: He won by a plurality : forty votes against thirty for each of his two opponents.

MANIA, PHOBIA

mania

A compulsive craving, enthusiasm or love for something.

Example: Some people have a mania for chocolates.

phobia

A compulsive fear of something.

Example: Dorothy has only one real phobia—spiders terrify her.

OPHTHALMOLOGIST, OCULIST, OPTICIAN, OPTOMETRIST

ophthalmologist

A physician who specialises in diseases of the eye.

Oculist is an older word for *ophthalmologist.*

optician

A person who makes or sells eyeglasses or other optical goods.

optometrist

A technician who measures visual ability and provides lenses for eyeglasses.

PERSECUTE, PROSECUTE

persecute

To oppress; to harass persistently.

Example: The Romans persecuted the early Christians.

prosecute

To try by law.

Example: The engineer of the wrecked train was prosecuted for criminal negligence.

SHALL, WILL

shall

The word is used with *I* and *we* to express the future tense of verbs.

Example: I shall be in Chennai next week.

We shall be in Chennai next week.

will

This word is used with *you, he, she, it* and *they* to express the future tense of verbs.

Example: You will be in Chennai next week.

SLANDER, LIBEL

slander

A spoken defamation or unjustified attack on a person's reputation.

Example: Three people heard him slander me by saying I can't hold down a job.

libel

A published written or broadcast defamation or unjustified attack on a person's reputation.

Example: A newspaper or TV commentator can be sued for libel.

STALAGMITE, STALACTITE

stalagmite

A tapering formation growing upward from the floor of a cave.

stalactite

A tapering formation hanging down from the roof of a cave.

STRATEGY, TACTICS

strategy

An overall campaign or plan.

Example: Our strategy was to concentrate on studies before turning our attention to sports.

tactics

Specific techniques and plays.

Example: Our sales tactics include daily newspaper advertising and 20 per cent discount offers.

UNCOMPARABLE, INCOMPARABLE

uncomparable

Not open to comparison; so different that comparison is impossible.

Example: Horses and aeroplanes are uncomparable.

incomparable

Unique; in a class by itself.

Example: Elvis Presley was an incomparable singer.

UNCONSCIOUS, SUBCONSCIOUS

unconscious

Not conscious, as a person who has fainted; or, totally unaware; or, that part of the mind not in the field of awareness.

Examples

1. Edna was unconscious for two hours after the accident.
2. The psychiatrist can probe the unconscious.

subconscious

Mental activity of which one is not aware, but which can sometimes be brought to the level of consciousness.

Examples

1. Oswald may have had a subconscious desire to injure his father.
2. A psychiatrist can help some people to understand their subconscious urges.

UNORGANISED, DISORGANISED

unorganised

Without any plan or order.

Example: An unorganised mob can accomplish nothing but chaos.

disorganised

Having a bad, misused or abandoned plan or order.

Example: The office, where everything had worked so smoothly, disorganised after Nitin left.

VERBAL, ORAL

verbal

Communication in words, whether spoken or written.

oral

Spoken as opposed to written communication.

Example: He chose to give his teacher an oral rather than a written report.

VOCATION, AVOCATION

vocation

A person's main work.

Example: Carpentry was his main vocation.

Avocation

A person's hobby or diversion.

Example: Stamp collection was his favourite avocation.

13

FOREIGN WORDS

English has constantly borrowed words and expressions from other languages. The following are the foreign words that have become popular in English usage.

ad hoc

Latin. Pertaining to this particular thing; designating a committee formed for a specific purpose in a specific situation.

Examples

1. We have appointed an ad hoc committee to deal with the affair.
2. Problems were solved on an ad hoc basis.

a priori

Latin. Prior to experience.

Example: A priori is applied to a mode of reasoning by which we proceed from the cause to the effect.

aficionado

Spanish. An enthusiast; a devotee, as a fan of bullfights.

Example: He was an aficionado of bullfighting.

àla carte

French. By the menu; applied to a meal in which each item on the menu has a separate price, as opposed to a complete meal for an all-in-one price.

Example: We only have an àla carte menu.

àla mode

French. In the latest fashion; specifically, with ice-cream on top (which was once a new way to serve pie and cake).

alter ego

Latin. A second self; a close friend; a confidant.

Example: He is my alter ego—we go everywhere together.

auf Wiedersehen

German. Till we meet again; goodbye.

Example: Thank you for coming, and auf wiedersehen.

bona fide

Latin. In good faith; genuine.

Example: On landing at the castle, they had to establish their bona fides.

cadenza

Italian. A musical flourish.

Example: Cadenza is an elaborate passage played by the soloist near the end of a movement in a concert.

canapè

French. A small piece of bread or a cracker, spread with cheese, caviar, etc., usually eaten as an appetiser.

Example: We indulged in canapa's just before dinner.

carte blanche

French. Unrestricted authority; permission to do whatever one wishes.

Example: I have given her carte blanche in the matter of her marriage.

coup d' etat

French. An unexpected stroke of policy; especially, a hidden seizure of Government.

Example: The army staged a *coup d'etat.*

crescendo

Italian. Increase in volume of sound.

Example: The advertising compaign reached a crescendo at Christmas.

cut-de-sac

French. A blind alley; a dead end.

Example: After many twists and turns, they reached a cul-de-sac.

cupola

Italian. A small dome.

Example: The cupola was studded with precious gems.

de facto

Latin. Existing in fact, with or without legal sanction.

Example: Though his kingship was challenged, he continued to rule *de facto.*

dossier

French. A collection of papers, documents, etc.

Example: He always carries his dossier with him when he travels abroad.

en rapport

French. In sympathetic relation or harmonious agreement.

Example: We are en rapport with the proposals of the committee.

esprit de corps

French. A spirit of devotion to one's group and its goals.

Example: The family believed in living a life of *esprit de corps.*

fete

French. A festival or outdoor entertainment.

Example: There was a school fete at the church grounds.

e'clat

French. Brilliance of action or effect; applause.

Example: Her latest novel was accepted with great e'clat.

fiasco

Italian. Humiliating failure.

Example: The party was a total fiasco because the wrong date was given on the invitations.

finesse

French. Tact or skill.

Example: He wheedled money from his father with considerable finesse.

gasconade

French. Bragging talk.

Example: This dislike him for his gasconade.

habiliments

French. Articles of clothing.

Example: His habiliments smell of cigar smoke.

inamorata

Italian. A beloved woman.

Example: His wife is an *inamorata.*

inferno

Italian. A hellish place.

Example: The place was a blazing inferno.

ingenue

French. A young woman of simplicity and innocence.

Example: She liked to play the part of an ingenue.

in toto

Latin. Totally; altogether.

Example: They occupied the building in toto.

flotilla

Spanish. A fleet of small ships.

Example: A destroyer flotilla was ready at the port for a war.

hauteur

French. Disdainful pride.

Example: His hauteur and egoism are obnoxious.

libretto

Italian. The text or words of an opera.

Example: He had composed a fine libretto for the new opera.

macabre

French. Gruesome.

Example: He narrated a macabre ghost story.

meti'er

French. A person's special calling.

Example: Don't ask me how to make an omelette; cooking is not my meti'er.

milieu

French. Environment.

Example: Coming from another milieu, she found life as an actress very strange at first.

non sequitur

Latin. An irrelevant remark or conclusion.

Example: This *non sequitur* invalidates his argument.

patois

French. A local dialect.

Example: He speaks the local *patois.*

piazza

Italian. A veranda, public square or market-place.

Example: There was a fairly big crowd gathered at the *piazza.*

portmanteau

French. Suitcase.

Example: He had a dozen shirts in his portmanteau.

potpourr'e

French. Medley or mixture.

Example: She had a collection of potpourri in the drawing room.

vendetta

Italian. A feud.

Example: We plan to wage a personal vendetta against the post office.

14

SPECIALISTS

In the vast field of physical care almost every part and function of the body has its own specialist or therapist. There are people specialised in other fields besides medice. Find out what each person is specialised in.

aerologist

A specialist in the branch of physics which treats the air, its constituent parts, properties and phenomena.

anaesthetist

A person trained to administer anaesthetics, as during an operation.

anthropologist

One who specialises in the study of the science of man and mankind.

archaeologist

A person skilled in the science of prehistoric antiquities, the history of peoples and the remains of their period.

artist

A person skilled in fine arts such as sculpture, painting, etc.

biologist

One who studies the science of life of animals and plants; including their morphology, physiology, origin, etc.

botanist

One who studies plants or vegetables, their structure, and generic and specific differences.

cardiologist

A doctor who specialises in the study of the heart and its functions.

chiropodist

A specialist in the minor ailments of the foot, including bunions, unicorns, etc. Also called a *podiatrist*.

chronologist

One versed in the science of ascertaining the true periods or years when past events or transactions took place, and arranging them in their proper order according to their dates.

conchologist

One who specialises in the field of zoology dealing with the nature, formation and classification of the shells of molluscs.

cosmologist

One well versed in the general science or theory of the cosmos or material universe, its parts, elements and laws.

dermatologist

A physician who specialises in treating diseases of the skin.

ecologist

A specialist in the branch of sociology concerned with human population, their environment, spatial distribution, and resulting cultural patterns.

economist

One versed in the science treating of production, distribution and consumption of wealth or the material welfare of mankind.

endocrinologist

A specialist in the science that deals with the endocrine glands and their relation to bodily changes and disease.

entomologist

A person who studies that branch of zoology which deals with the structure, habits and classification of insect.

environmentalist

A specialist dealing in all the physical, social and cultural factors and conditions influencing the existence of an organism or its development.

epistemologist

One who studies the theory of origin, nature, methods and limits of knowledge.

eschatologist

A person who studies the doctrine of the last or final things, as death, judgment, and the destination of the soul.

ethologist

One who studies the science of ethics or human character formation, and the study of animal behaviour.

etymologist

One well versed in the branch of philology concerned with the origin and history of words.

geologist

A person skilled in the science that deals with the physical history and structure of the earth, and the physical changes which it has undergone.

graphologist

One who studies handwriting, especially for analysis of the writer's character.

gynaecologist

A doctor who specialises in the care of woman, especially in matters concerning the reproductive organs.

haematologist

One who deals with that branch of medicine concerned with the blood and its diseases.

herbalist

A person who collects plants and deals in medicinal plants; also a healer who specialises in the curative properties of herbs.

herpetologist

One skilled in the branch of study which has to do with reptiles and amphibians.

histologist

One who studies plant and animal tissues, especially of their microscopic structures.

horologist

A person dealing with the science of measuring time, and the art of constructing machines for measuring time.

horticulturist

One who is skilled in the science and art of cultivating flowers, herbs, shrubs, fruits and garden negetables.

hydrologist

A specialist in the science that treats the properties, laws and distribution of water underground, on the earth's surface, and in the atmosphere.

ichthyologist

One who studies a branch of zoology dealing with fishes.

internist

A doctor who specialises in the large, general branch of medicine called internal medicine.

lapidarist

A craftsman who cuts, polishes, and engraves gems or precious stones.

linguist

A person skilled in languages, and one who knows several languages.

meteorologist

One who deals with the science concerned with atmospheric phenomena, especially in relation to weather and climate.

naturalist

One versed in natural history or natural science, and making a study of animals and plants.

neurologist

A doctor who specialises in treating disorders of the nervous system.

obstetrician

A doctor who specialises in delivering babies and in medical problems related to childbirth.

oculist

One trained and skilled in the examination and treatment of the eye.

oenologist

A person specialised in the science of wine making.

ololaryngologist

A specialist in the branch of medicine which is concerned with the ear, nose and throat.

ontologist

A specialist in the medical science that treats and studies tumours and cancer.

ophthalmologist

A doctor who specialises in the anatomy, functions and diseases of the eye.

ornithologist

A specialist in that branch of zoology which treats of the form, structure, classification and habits of birds.

orthodontist

A dentist who specialises in preventing and correcting irregularities of the teeth, such as crooked or otherwise defective teeth.

orthopaedist

A doctor who specialises in correcting deformities of the skeletal system and treating diseases of the bones, spine, joints, muscles, etc.

osteologist

A doctor who deals with that branch of anatomy which is concerned with bones and their structure.

paediatrician

A doctor who specialises in the care and treatment of babies and young children.

palae-ethnologist

A person specialised in the branch of ethnology that treats the earliest or most primitive races of mankind.

palaebotanist

One who specialises in the study of plants found in the fossil state.

palaeographist

A person specialised in the science of deciphering ancient documents or inscriptions.

palaeontologist

One well versed in that branch of biological science which treats fossil remains.

palaeozoologist

A specialist dealing with the nature of diseases, their causes, symptoms and effects on the organism.

pharmacologist

A specialist in the science of drugs, or the art of preparing medicines.

physiologist

A specialist in the science dealing with the normal functions of living plant and animal organisms or their organs.

physiotherapist

A specialist in the treatment of disease, bodily weaknesses, or defects by physical remedies, such as massage and exercise.

pisciculturist

A specialist dealing with the breeding, rearing, preservation, and feeding of fish by artificial means.

podiatrist

A therapist whose speciality is treating ailments of the feet.

psephologist

One who specialises in the study of elections, including voting trends and systems.

psychiatrist

A physician specialising in the field of medicine that deals with the diagnosis and treatment of emotional and mental disorders.

psychologist

One versed in the branch of knowledge which deals with the human mind.

radiologist

A specialist in the science that treats of the properties, laws and distribution of water underground, on the earth's surface, and in the atmosphere.

seismologist

A specialist in the science of the origin, development and characteristics of vibrations in the earth, primarily those generated by earthquakes but also including vibrations made by man-made explosions and weather conditions.

sericulturist

One who specialises in the breeding and treatment of silkworms for producing raw silk.

silviculturist

One who is specialised in the filed of forestry, cultivation and care of trees in a forest.

sinologist

One who is specialised in the study of China, including its language, literature and history.

strategist

One skilled in the science of forming and carrying out military operations.

taxidermist

A specialist skilled in the art of treating, stuffing and mounting the skins of animals so that they retain their natural appearance.

telelologist

One skilled in the steady of evidence in nature indicating that final causes exist.

urologist

A specialist in the field of medicine devoted to the study, diagnoses and treatment of any malfunction or disease of the urinary tract.

ventriloquist

One skilled in the art of producing voice sounds so that they seem to come from a person or place at a distance from the speaker.

virologist

A specialist in the science which deals with viruses and the diseases they cause.

zoologist

One specialised in the science that deals with the endocrine glands and their relation to bodily changes and disease.

15

ODDBALLS

There are many words that describe types of people and the ways they react to the world about them. The following words deal with human behaviour, both normal and abnormal.

aesthete

A person who is devoted to beauty in nature, art, painting, music, etc.; or, a person who displays an extravagant or affected admiration for beauty and the arts.

altruist

A person who is selflessly concerned with the welfare of others; one who puts the comfort and happiness of others before his own.

ascetic

A person who leads a simple, austere life, avoiding luxury and pleasure, seeking solitude, practising self-discipline, and devoting himself to contemplation or meditation.

battleaxe

A woman with a bad temper or domineering nature especially a wife.

conservative

A person who wants to preserve the existing order of things, feeling content or safe with things as they are.

exhibitionist

A show-off; a person who tries to attract attention to himself by exaggerated or inappropriate behaviour.

hussy

A cheeky or frivolous girl, or a vulgar or promiscuous woman.

hypochondriac

A person who worries constantly—usually without any real reason—about the state of his health, believing that he has many ailments, taking extreme health precautions, etc.

kleptomaniac

A person who has an irresistible desire to steal and shoplift—not because he is in need of what he steals, but because stealing gives him an emotional satisfaction.

megalomaniac

A person who suffers from delusions of greatness.

optimist

A person who tends to look on the bright side of things, or one who tends to think that the world is basically good and that what happens is for the best.

paranoid

A person who believes that other people are always plotting against him, cheating and persecuting him, feeling hate for him, etc.

pessimist

A person who tends to look on the darker side of things, or one who believes that the world is basically bad or evil.

pragmatist

A person who believes that ideas have value only in terms of their practical consequence and that practical results are the sole test of the truth or validity of beliefs.

realist

A person who believes in basing his life on facts and who dislikes anything that seems imaginary, impractical, theoretical or utopian.

16

FROM THE ART WORLD

Painting, sculpture and drawing have a special vocabulary of their own. Given below are some useful terms that you can add to your vocabulary.

abstract

A painting that does not portray objects or figures, but uses lines, masses of colour, and geometrical forms such as oblongs, aqures, circles, etc.

bas-relief

A piece of sculpture in which the figures are raised out only slightly from a background panel or wall, such as a frieze on a building.

chairoscuro

The distribution and treatment of light and shade in a picture; or, a kind of picture using only light and shade and no definite lines.

etching

A process for forming a design or drawing on a metal plate from which an inkimpression on paper can be taken.

fresco

A painting made by applying colours to a wet plaster surface, so that they sink in deeply and dry with it.

frieze

A long strip or band of decoration, as on a building, ornamented with lettering, sculpture, scrolls, etc.

gouache

A painting using opaque colours mixed with water and gum.

impasto

A method of painting in which colours are applied thickly so that they stand out from the canvas.

impressionism

A late nineteenth-century theory and style of painting that tried to produce the visual impression of the subject with the colour values of light and air—sometimes purposely resulting in paintings that seem nasty or vaguely out of focus.

landscape

A painting representing a tract of country with the varcous objects it contains.

mobile

A piece of sculpture made of wire, strips of metal, etc., in such a way that it moves when touched or blown by the wind.

mural

A painting applied directly to a wall or ceiling.

oil colour

Paint made by grinding a pigment in oil, most often linseed oil.

palette

A flat, thin piece of wood, plastic, etc., which holds the different paints used by an artist, and which is often held in the hand.

pastel

A drawing made with coloured crayons, especially soft crayons made of pipe clay, pigment and gum water.

portrait

A painted picture or representation of a person.

study

A preliminary sketch or exercise, as a preliminary rough sketch of an object or landscape that will later be the subject of a painting.

tempera

A fast-drying paint made of colours that are mixed with water and egg yolk; or, a painting made from such paint.

water colour

A painting made with pigments mixed in water; or, paint having water as the medium.

17

DIMINUTIVES

English has a number of suffixes called diminutives; they show that the word to which they are attached refers to a miniature-sized version of the object. The diminutive suffixes are :

cle, cule, el, et (or *ette), i, let, ling* and *ule.*

baronet

A British hereditary knight, rank next below a baron, not entitled to a seat in the House of Lords. From old French, diminutive of *baron.*

booklet

A small book.

bracelets

An ornamental band or chain encircling the wrist. Old French, diminutive of *bracel,* literally, a little arm, hence an armband or bracelet.

bumpkins

Country dwellers, viewed by others as being unsophisticated. Probably from Middle Dutch *boomken,* a squat person, dominative of *boom,* a tree.

capsule

Literally, a small box; hence, a small soluble container for enclosing a dose of medicine; or, a small, detachable compartment of an aeroplane or spacecraft.

cigarette

Literally, a small cigar; hence, a small roll of finely cut tobacco for smoking, wrapped in a cylinder of paper.

codicil

Literally, a small writing tablet; hence, a supplement to a will, changing or explaining something; an addition. A codicil is so called because it is brief.

corpuscles

Cells capable of free movement rather than fixed in tissue, especially blood cells. Latin *corpusculum,* diminutive of *corpus,* a body.

darling

Literally, little dear (*dar* is an ancient variant spelling of *dear*); hence, a person tenderly loved.

duckling

A young duck.

globule

Literally, a small globe; hence, a tiny sphere of matter or drop of liquid.

gosling

A young goose.

granules

Small, solid particles of a substance. From Late Latin *granum,* grain; related to *grain.*

islet

A small island.

leaflet

Literally, a small leaf, as a leaf of folded paper; hence, a small printed sheet of paper or a brochure.

mannikin

A model of the human body, used for study in art and medical schools. Middle Dutch *mannekin*, diminutive of *man*, a man; related to *mannequin* (originally a French form), a tailor's dummy or model for clothes.

molecule

Literally, a small mass; hence, the smallest particle of an element or compound that can exist separately without losing its physical or chemical properties.

morsel

Literally, a small bite; hence, a small piece of anything.

particle

A small part or piece of matter; a speck; or, a very small amount.

pullet

A young hen, usually less than one year old. From old French *poulet, pallet*, diminutive of *Paul* or *poul*, a chicken, from Latin *pullus*, the young of an animal.

reticule

A old-fashioned handbag, typically made of netted fabric, and closed with a drawstring. French, from Latin *reticulum*, diminutive of *rete*, a net.

rosettes

Ornamental badges made of ribbons gathered into the shape of a rose. French, literally, small roses, from French *rosa*, a rose.

suckling

Literally, an unweaned young animal or child; hence, an unweaned mammal; or, an infant or very young child.

underling

A subordinate treated as unimportant. Middle English *under*+suffix *ling*, small or inferior.

18

Words from Everywhere

Over the last 400 years, as British influence has spread around the world, through trade and the acquiring of a vast overseas empire in the eighteenth and nineteenth centuries, English has taken in words from just about every language it has come into contact with. Some of these words have been adopted directly; others have come into English via one of the European languages.

Here are some of the words borrowed at various times. It will give you an idea of the extraordinary variety that English has to offer.

SCOTS AND GAELIC

banshee

Female spirit with a distinctive wail, thought by some to warn of death in a house.

bard

Poet.

blarney

Smooth talk that flatters and deceives people.

bog

Net spongy ground formed of decaying vegetation.

brat

A badly-behaved child.

cadge

Get or try to get something from somebody by asking, often unreasonably.

galore

In plenty.

plaid

Long piece of woollen cloth, worn over the shoulders by Scottish highlanders; or, cloth, usually with a tartan pattern, used for this, and for kilts, etc.

slogan

Word or phrase that is easy to remember, used as a motto, e.g., by a political party or in advertising.

smithereens

Small pieces of fragments; bits.

spree

Lively and enjoyable outing, usually with much spending of money.

Tory

Member of the British Conservative Party.

trousers

Outer garment covering both legs and reaching from the waist to the ankles.

whisky

Strong alcoholic drink distilled from matted grain, especially barley or rye.

WELSH

coracle

A small light boat made of wickerwork and covered with watertight materials, used by fishermen on Welsh and Irish rivers and lakes.

corgi

Small breed of Welsh dog.

flannel

Type of soft loosely women woollen cloth.

flummery

Oatmeal or flour boiled with water until thick; a sweet dessert, especially a moulded cold pudding, usually served with a fruit sauce. Also means an empty compliment.

MODERN FRENCH

à la carte

According to the bill of fare; with a stated price for each dish.

ballet

A classical dance, more or less elaborate, in which several persons take part and create a certain expression by particular movements.

bete noire

A bugbear; an object of one's special dread or aversion.

brochure

A booklet of salient facts on a subject.

camouflage

The act of disguising or concealing naturally troops or equipment as by the use of paint, smoke screens, or branches; a pretence, disguise, manner or plan intended as a false front.

chic

Fashion know-how, easy elegance and tasteful, distinctive style.

cliche

A hackneyed word, phrase or idea.

coup d'etat

A sudden and decisive measure in politics, especially one effecting a change of government illegally or by force.

cul-de-sac

A street, lane or other passage closed at one end.

elite

Those who are choice or elect.

etiquette

Prescribed or accepted code of usage in matters of ceremony, as at a court, in official or other formal observances, or in polite society generally.

fait accompli

Thing already done, that cannot be done and is therefore not worth arguing about.

garage

A place for sheltering or repairing motor vehicles.

gourmet

A connoisseur of food and drink.

hors d'oeuvre

An appetiser or relish.

liaison

Communication and cooperation between units of an organisation; person who liaises.

menu

A bill of fare; a list of meals that can be served.

naive

Natural and innocent in speech and behaviour; too ready to

believe what one is told; showing lack of experience or judgement.

nouveau riche

Person who has recently, and often suddenly, become rich, especially one who displays his wealth ostentatiously.

pâtè

Rich paste made of finely minced meat or fish.

police

Official organisation whose job is to keep public order, prevent and solve crimes, etc.

prestige

Respect based on good reputation, past achievements, etc.; power to impress others, especially as a result of wealth, distinction, etc.

rendezvous

Meeting at an agreed time.

ricochet

Strike a surface and rebound at an angle.

suede

Type of soft leather with one side rubbed so that it has a soft roughened surface.

verve

Enthusiasm, spirit or vigour, especially in artistic or literary work.

SPANISH

canyon

Deep gorge, usually with a river flowing through it.

cockroach

Large, dark-brown insect that infests kitchens and bathrooms.

macho

Aggressively masculine.

rodeo

Rounding up of cattle on a ranch for branding, etc.; exhibition or contest of comboy's skill in lassoing and riding cattle, untamed horses, etc.

PORTUGUESE

albino

Person or animal born with no colouring pigment in the skin and hair, and the eyes (which are pink).

corral

Enclosure for horses, cattle, etc., on a ranch or farm; defensive circle of wagons, etc.

marmalade

Type of jam made from citrus fruit, especially oranges.

rusk

Type of biscuit or bread baked hard and crisp, especially one used for feeding babies.

DUTCH

boss

Person who controls or gives orders to workers; manager; employer.

brandy

Strong alcoholic drink distilled from wine or fermented fruit juice.

coleslaw

Finely shredded raw cabbage mixed with dressing and eaten as a salad.

cruise

Sail boat, either for pleasure or, in wartime, looking for enemy ships; travel at a moderate speed, using fuel efficiently; drive a vehicle at a moderate speed.

drill

Tool or machine with a detachable pointed end for making holes; training in military exercises; thorough training by practical and usually repetitive exercises.

gin

Colourless alcoholic drink distilled from grain or malt and favoured with juniper berries, often used in cocktails.

groove

Long narrow cut or depression in the surface of hard material; spiral cut on a gramophone disc for the needle or stylus.

hoist

Raise by means of ropes, special apparatus, etc.

kit

Clothing and personal equipment of a soldier, etc., or a traveller; equipment needed for a particular activity, situation or trade.

loiter

Stand by idly.

luck

Chance, especially thought of as a force that brings good or bad fortune.

poppycock

Nonsense.

skate

Either of a pair of boots with still blades fixed to the soles so that the wearer can glide smoothly over ice; move on skates.

sledge

Vehicle with long narrow strips of wood, metal, etc, instead of wheels, for travelling over ice and snow.

splinter

Small, thin, sharp piece of wood, metal, glass, etc., broken off a larger piece.

split

Cause something to break or be broken into two or more parts, especially from end to end.

waffle

Talk or write, especially at great length, without saying anything very important or sensible; small crisp cake made of cooked batter with pattern of squares on it, often eaten with syrup.

wagon

Four-wheeled vehicle for carrying heavy goods, usually pulled by horses or oxen; open railway carriage.

AFRIKAANS

aardvark

A large South African quadruped with strong claws, an extensible tongue, large ears and tail, which feeds principally on ants and termites.

apartheid

Racial segregation, separating Europeans and non-Europeans.

boer

African of Dutch decent.

commandeer

Take possession or control of vehicles, buildings, etc. forcibly or for official military purposes.

commando

Member of a group of soldiers specially trained for carrying out quick raids in enemy areas.

trek

Long, hard journey, especially on foot.

veld

Flat, treeless, open grassland of the South African plateau.

GERMAN

blitz

Sudden intensive military attack, especially from the air.

delicatessen

Shop selling prepared foods, often unusual or imported, ready for serving.

dollar

Unit of money.

kindergarten

School for very young children.

kitsch

Cheap and showy vulgarity or pretentiousness in art, design, etc.

lager

Type of light, pale beer.

nickel

Chemical element, a hard silver-white metal often used in alloys.

rucksack

Bag strapped to the back from the shoulders, used by hikers, climbers, etc.

snorkel

Tube that allows a swimmer to take in air while under water; device that allows a submarine to take in air while under water.

spanner

Tool for gripping and turning nuts on crews, bolts, etc.

swindle

Cheat somebody, especially in business transaction.

waltz

Ballroom dance for couples with a graceful flowing melody in triple time.

zinc

Chemical element, a bluish-white used in alloys and to cover iron sheets, wire, etc. As a protection against rust.

YIDDISH

chutzpah

Supreme self-confidence.

nosh

Food; quick meal, snack, etc.

SCANDINAVIAN

fjord (also fiord)

Long, narrow inlet of the sea between high cliffs, as in Norway.

geyser

Column of hot water or steam sent up from the ground at intervals, caused by the heating; apparatus used for heating large amounts of water in a kitchen or batroom.

mink

Small stoat-like animal of the weasel family; coat made from this fur.

ombudsman

Official appointed by a government to investigate and report on complaints made by citizens against public authorities.

rug

Thick floor-mat (usually smaller than a carpet); piece of thick, warm fabric used as a blanket or covering.

saga

Long story of heroic deeds, especially of Icelandic or Norwegian heroes; story of a long series of events or adventures, especially one involving several generations of people.

ski

Either of a pair of long narrow strips of wood, plastic, etc, fixed to a person's boots so that he can glide smoothly over snow.

walrus

Large sea-animal living in the Arctic regions, similar to a seal but having two long tusks.

CZECH

howitzer

Short gun for firing shells at a high angle and at short range.

pistol

Type of small gun, held and fired with one hand.

robot

Machine that can perform the actions of a person, operated automatically or by remote control.

HUNGARIAN

coach

Bus for carrying passengers over long distances; carriage; large four-wheeled carriage pulled by horses and used for carrying passengers.

goulash

Dish of Hungarian origin consisting of stewed beef seasoned with paprika.

hussar

Soldier of a cavalry regiment, carrying light weapons.

sabre

Heavy cavalry sword with a curved blade; light sword with a tapering blade, used in fencing.

RUSSIAN

balalaika

Musical instrument like a guitar with a triangular body and three strings, popular in Slav countries.

commissar

Formerly, head of a Government department in the USSR; formerly office in the army of the *USSR* giving political instruction glasnost.

knout

A whip with leather thongs, used formerly in Russia to punish criminals.

mammoth

An extinct species of Pleistocene elephant with long tusks and covered with dense, shaggy hair, the remains of which are found buried in Europe, Asia and North America; very large; enormous; gigantic.

perestroika

Restructuring of the society economic and political system.

pogrom

Organised persecution or killing of a particular group or class of people, especially because of their race or religion.

samovar

Container for heating water used especially in Russia for making tea.

TURKISH

bosh

Nonsense.

caviare

Pickled roe of sturgeon or other large fish, eaten as a delicacy.

coffee

Powder obtained by grinding the roasted seeds of the coffee plant; a drink made by adding hot water to ground or powdered coffee.

horde

Very large group; huge crowd; throng.

kebab

Small pieces of meat and vegetables cooked and often served on a skewer.

kiosk

Small open structure where newspapers, refreshments, etc. are sold; public telephone box or booth.

yogurt

Slightly sour, thick liquid food, consisting of milk fermented by added bacteria and often flavoured with fruit, etc.

ARABIC

admiral

Naval officer of high rank; officer commanding a fleet or squadron.

cipher

Method of secret writing in which a set of letters or symbols is used to represent other; code; key to a secret message; the symbol 0 representing rough or zero.

crimson

Deep red.

ghoul

In stories, spirit that robs graves and feeds on the corpses in them; person with an unaturally strong interest in death, disaster and other unpleasant things.

harem

Separate part of a traditional Muslim house in which the women live; women living in this.

hazard

Thing that can cause hunger; risk.

lute

Stringed musical instrument with a pear-shaped body, used mainly from the fourteenth to the eighteenth centuries and by plucking with the fingers.

magazine

Store for arms, ammunition, explosives, etc.; chamber holding the cartidges of a rifle or pistol before they are fed into the breech; place that holds the roll or cartridge of film in a camera; paper-covered periodical, usually weekly or monthly, with articles, stories etc. by various writers.

masquerade

False show; pretence.

racket

Loud noise; uproar or noisy disturbance; illegal or dishonest way of getting money; business or occupation; bat with a round or oval stringed frame, used for playing in tennis, badminton, etc.

saffron

Bright orange strands obtained from the flowers of the autumn crocus, used in cooking.

sash

Long strip of cloth worn around the waist or over one shoulder as an ornament or as part of a uniform; either of a pair of window frames, one above the other, opening and closing by sliding up and down in grooves.

sherbet

Refreshing drink of weak sweet fruit juice; sweet fizzy drink, or the powder from which it is made.

tariff

List of fixed charges, especially for rooms, meals, etc. At a hotel; duty to be paid on imports or less often exports.

zero

Rough; nil; lowest point; none; nothing at all.

PERSIAN

bazaar

Group of shops or stalls or part of a town where these are; place where there is a sale of goods to raise money for charitable purposes.

candy

Sugar hardened by repeated boiling; sweets or chocolate.

caravan

Large vehicle on wheels, equipped for luring in and usually towed by a motor vehicle; covered cart or wagon; group of people travelling together across the desert.

check

Make sure of something by examining or investigating it; slow down or stop.

divan

Long, low couch without a back or arms.

jackal

Wild animal of Africa and Asia that is related to the dog.

jasmine

Shrub with white or yellow sweet-smelling flowers..

lemon

Oral yellow fruit with acidic juice used for drinks and flavouring.

lilac

Shrub with sweet-smelling pale purple or white blossom.

magic

Power of apparently using supernatural forces to change the form of things or influence events; superstitious practices based on this; tricks with mysterious results, done to entertain; charming or encharting quality.

orange

Round, thick-skinned juicy edible fruit that is a reddish-yellow colour when ripe.

paradise

Heaven; ideal or perfect place; state of perfect happiness.

shawl

Large piece of material worn round the shoulders or head of a woman, or wrapped round a baby.

spinach

Type of common garden plant with wide dark green leaves that are cooked and eaten as a vegetable.

talc (or talcum)

Smooth soft mineral that is powdered for use as a lubricant or powder.

tulip

Garden plant growing from a bulb in spring, with a large, brightly-coloured, cup-shaped flower on a tall-stem.

turban

Men's headdress (worn especially by Muslims and Sikhs) made by winding a length of cloth tightly round the head; woman's close-fitting hat resembling this.

INDIAN

bangle

Large decorative ring worn round the arm or ankle.

bungalow

small house with one storey.

chintz

Type of usually glazed cotton with a printed design, used for curtains, furniture covers, etc.

chit

Young child; small or thin young woman; short written note or letter; note showing an amount of money owed.

cot

Bed for a young child, usually with sides to prevent the child falling out; simple, narrow bed.

cushy

Not requiring much effort.

dinghy

Any of various types of small open boat; inflatable rubber boat.

jungle

Area of land, usually in a tropical country, that is covered with a thick growth of trees and tangled plants; disordered mass of things.

booty

Goods taken from an enemy in war, or stolen by thieves.

mongoose

Small furry tropical mammal that kills snakes, birds, rats, etc.

mulligatawny

Thick, highly seasoned soup with curry powder in it.

pariah

Social outcast.

pyjamas

Loose-fitting jacket and trousers worn for sleeping in, especially by men; loose trousers tied round the waist, worn by Muslims and others of both sexes in India and Pakistan.

shampoo

Soapy liquid, cream, etc., for washing the hair.

thug

Criminal or hooligan.

toddy

Alcoholic drink made of spirits, sugar and hot water.

verandah

Roofed open-fronted terrace or platform which extends from the front, back or sides of a house, sports pavilion, etc.

MALAY

amok

Rush about in a wild and angry frenzy.

bamboo

Tall plant of the grass family with hard, hollow jointed stems that are used for making canes, furniture, etc.

caddy (tea)

Box in which tea is kept for daily use.

gingham

Cotton or linen cloth with a striped or checked pattern.

gong

Metal disc that gives a resonant note when struck with a stick, used especially as a musical instrument or as a signal for meals.

launch (motor)

Large motor boat.

paddy

Field where rice is grown; rice that is still growing or in the truck.

sago

Starchy food in the form of hard white grains, used in puddings, obtained from the pith of a type of palm-tree.

CHINESE

ketchup

Thick sauce made from tomatoes, vinegar, etc. and used as cold seasoning.

kowtow

Be submissive, humble or respectful.

kung fu

Form of unarmed combat similar to karate.

silk

Fine soft thread produced by silkworms to make their cocoons; thread or cloth made from this.

soya

Type of bean rich in protein, grown for food and used especially as a substitute for meat.

tea

Dried leaves of an evergreen shrub, which are used for making a drink by pouring boiling water on these leaves.

typhoon

Violent tropical hurricane that occurs in the pacific.

wok

Large pan shaped like a bowl, used for cooking especially Chinese food.

JAPANESE

bonsai

A potted tree or shrub-like plant which has been dwarfed by special methods of culture.

judo

Sport of wrestling and self-defence between two people who try to throw each other to the ground.

kamikaze

Japanese aircraft deliberately crashed on enemy ships, etc.

karate

System of armed combat in which the hands, feet, etc. are used as weapons.

kimono

Long, loose Japanese robe with side sleeves, worn with a sash.

origami

The Japanese art of folding paper into various realistic or decorative shapes.

rickshaw

Light two-or three-wheeled covered vehicle, pulled or ridden by men.

tycoon

Wealthy and powerful businessman or industrialist.

AUSTRALIAN

boomerang

Curved flat wooden missile which can be thrown so that it returns to the thrower if it fails to hit anything; action or remark that causes unexpected harm to the person responsible for it.

budgerigar

Type of Australian parakeet, often used as a cage-bird.

dingo

Wild Australian dog.

kangaroo

Australian animal that jumps along on its strong hind legs, the female carrying its young in a pouch on the front of its body.

wallaby

Various types of small kangaroo.

POLYNESIAN

kiwi

New Zealand bird that cannot fly, with a long bill, short wings and no tail.

mana

A belief held by Polynesians that a power of supernatural origin may reside in a person or an object.

taboo

Among the Polynesians and other races of the south Pacific Ocean, separated or set apart as sacred, forbidden to general use, or placed under a prohibition or ban; ostracism.

tattoo

The act or practice of marking the skin with indelible patterns, pictures or legends by making punctures in it and inserting pigments.

ukulele

A musical instrument, usually four-stringed similar to a guitar but smaller in size.

AFRICAN

banana

Long thick-skinned edible fruit that is yellow when ripe.

banjo

Stringed musical instrument with a long neck and a round body, played by plucking with fingers.

chimpanzee

A type of small African ape.

cola

West African tree.

guinea

Formerly in Britain a gold coin worth the sum of 21 shillings used in stating professional fees, prices, etc.

okra

Tropical plant with green seed pods eaten as a vegetable.

raffia

Soft fibre from the leaves of palm-tree, used for tying up plants, weaving table mats, etc.

voodoo

Form of religion based on belief in witchcraft and magical rites, practised by blacks, especially in Haiti.

yam

Edible starchy tuber of a tropical climbing plant.

zombie

Dead body that has been brought to life by witchcraft; dull lifeless person who seems to act without thinking or not to be aware of what is happening around him; automaton.

ESKIMO

anorak

Usually waterproof hooded jacket worn as a protection against rain, wind and cold.

igloo

Small dome-shaped house built by Eskimos from blocks of hard snow as a temporary shelter.

kayak

Small covered canoe made of light wood covered with sealskins.

parka

Jacket made from skin and with a hood, worn by Eskimos.

NORTH AMERICAN INDIAN

chipmunk

Small striped required-like North American animal.

hickory

North American tree with edible nuts.

moccasin

Flat-soled shoe made from soft leather, as originally worn by north American Indians.

moose

Elk.

powwow

Meeting or conference of North American Indians; meeting to discuss something.

raccoon

Small North American flesh-eating mammal with a pointed snout and a bushy black-ringed tail.

skunk

Smelly bushy-tailed North American animal that can send out a strong impleasant smell as a defence when attached.

toboggan

Long light narrow sledge, often curved upwards at the front, used for sliding downhill on snow.

tomahawk

Light axe used as a tool or weapon by North American Indians.

totem

Natural object, especially an animal, considered by North American Indians as the emblem of a clan or family.

AZTEC

avocado

Pear-shaped tropical fruit.

cocoa

Dark brown powder made from crushed cacao sees; powdered chocolate.

chilli

Small pod of a type of paper plant, often dried or made into powder and used to give a hot taste to food.

chocolate

Brown edible substance in the form of powder or a block, made from roasted and crushed cacao seeds.

coyote

Small wolf of the plains of western North America.

tomato

Soft juicy red or yellow fruit eaten raw or cooked as a vegetable.

CARIBBEAN

barbecue

Outparty party at which food is cooked over an open fire in a metal frame.

cannibal

Person who eats human flesh; animal that eats its own kind.

hammock

Bed made of canvas or rope netting, suspended by cords at the ends, used especially on board ship.

hurricane

Storm with a violent wind, especially a West Indian cyclone.

maize

Tall cereal plant bearing yellow grain on large ears.

tobacco

Type of leaves that are dried, cured and used for smoking in pipes, cigarettes and cigars or chewing, or as snuff.

SOUTH AMERICAN

alpaca

Type of South American llama with long wool.

cashew

Tropical tree with its small edible kindney-shaped nut.

cocaine

Drug used as a local anaesthetic by doctors, and as a stimulant by drug addicts.

condor

Type of large vulture found mainly in South America.

guano

Dung from sea-birds, poultry, etc. used as a fertiliser.

jaguar

Large spotted member of the cat family inhabiting parts of central America.

toucan

Tropical American bird with brightly coloured feathers and a very large beak.